Welcome to "Who Am I? Unveiling History's Icons Through Clues," a quiz book crafted to ignite your curiosity and challenge your knowledge about some of the most influential figures in history. This book is a journey through time, providing glimpses into the lives and accomplishments of legendary personalities from various fields, including politics, music, science, and more.

Each quiz question in this book offers a series of clues that gradually reveal the identity of a famous individual. Your task is to piece together these hints and guess the person's name. This isn't just about what you know; it's about how well you can connect the dots and uncover the story behind each clue.

Here's how it works:

1. **Read the Clues Carefully:** Each question starts with a brief description that includes key facts, achievements, and interesting tidbits about the person in question.

2. **Think Broadly:** Consider the broader context of the clues. For example, a clue about leading a nation through a major war narrows down the possibilities significantly.

3. **Make Connections:** Use your knowledge of history, culture, and notable events to link the clues together. Sometimes, a single word or phrase can be the key to unlocking the answer.

4. **Guess the Identity:** Once you've gathered enough information from the clues, take your best guess. Don't worry if you're unsure; the goal is to learn and enjoy the process.

Be sure to have pen and paper ready as you work through each question. The answer will follow the clues.

Let's embark on this adventure together, uncovering the stories of those who have shaped our world. With each question, you'll delve deeper into the lives of these remarkable individuals, gaining insights and appreciation for their contributions.

So, turn the page, and let's get started! Who am I? Let the clues guide you to the answer.

"History will be kind to me for I intend to write it." –
Winston Churchill

Contents

Famous Directors	4
American Presidents	11
American Singers	17
British/Irish Singers	23
Cold War Figures	29
Famous Kings and Queens	34
Famous Scientists	38
Famous Actors	44
American Bands	51
British and Irish Bands	56
Famous Philosophers	62
Famous Characters from the Movies	67
American Sitcom Characters	75
British Sitcom Characters	82
Comedians	86
Fashion Designers	93
Dictators	98
American Historical Figures	104
Infamous Serial Killers	107
World Leaders (2000s-Present)	111
Ancient Era (Prehistoric Era pre-600 B.C.E.)	115
Classical Era to Middle Ages (600 B.C.E. to 1500 C.E.)	122
Age of Exploration to Pre-World War I (1500-1914)	128
Between the Wars and World War II (1914-1945)	134
IMDb's Top 30 Films - Famous Films	139
Famous Music Artists (Top Grammy Winners)	148
Famous Authors	153
Word Associations	160
Quotable Quest	164
Lateral Thinking Puzzles	171

Who Am I?

Famous Directors

Round 1: Easy

1. I am known for my distinctive style and influence in the thriller genre. Some of my most famous films include "Psycho," "Rear Window," and "Vertigo." My cameo appearances in my own films became one of my trademarks.

Who am I?

2. I am a visionary director famous for my work in science fiction and fantasy. My notable films include "E.T. the Extra-Terrestrial," "Jurassic Park," and "Indiana Jones." I co-founded Amblin Entertainment and DreamWorks.

Who am I?

3. I am a director celebrated for my films about crime and the Italian-American experience. My famous works include "Goodfellas," "Taxi Driver," and "The Wolf of Wall Street." I frequently collaborate with actor Robert De Niro.

Who am I?

4. I revolutionized the horror genre with my groundbreaking film "Halloween." I am also known for "The Thing" and "Escape from New York." My films often feature eerie synth scores that I compose myself.

Who am I?

5. I am an acclaimed director who has mastered both historical drama and epic fantasy. My filmography includes "Schindler's List," "Saving Private Ryan," and "The Lord of the Rings" trilogy, where I played a key role as a producer.

Who am I?

Round 2: Medium

6. I am a celebrated Japanese director known for my samurai epics and influence on Western cinema. My notable films include "Seven Samurai," "Rashomon," and "Ikiru." My storytelling and visual style have inspired many filmmakers worldwide.

Who am I?

7. I am an auteur known for my unique visual style and dark themes. My films include "Edward Scissorhands," "Beetlejuice," and "The Nightmare Before Christmas." I often collaborate with actor Johnny Depp and composer Danny Elfman.

Who am I?

8. I am a critically acclaimed director whose work often explores human emotions and social issues. My famous films include "Brokeback Mountain," "Life of Pi," and "Crouching Tiger, Hidden Dragon." I have received multiple Academy Awards.

Who am I?

9. I am an innovative director known for my complex narratives and mind-bending visuals. My notable works include "Inception," "The Dark Knight," and "Interstellar." My films often feature practical effects and minimal CGI.

Who am I?

10. I am an iconic director known for my groundbreaking work in silent films and early talkies. My famous films include "The Gold Rush," "City Lights," and "Modern Times." My character "The Tramp" is one of the most recognizable figures in cinema history.

Who am I?

Round 3: Hard

11. I am a French New Wave director known for my unconventional storytelling and editing techniques. My notable films include "Breathless," "Alphaville," and "Contempt." My work has had a lasting impact on the film industry.

Who am I?

12. I am a Mexican filmmaker acclaimed for my visually stunning and thematically rich films. My works include "Pan's Labyrinth," "The Shape of Water," and "Crimson Peak." My fascination with monsters and fantasy often permeates my films.

Who am I?

13. I am an Iranian director known for my minimalist and poetic style. My famous films include "Taste of Cherry," "Close-Up," and "The Wind Will Carry Us." I am regarded as one of the most influential filmmakers in world cinema.

Who am I?

14. I am a British director known for my gritty crime dramas and complex narratives. My famous works include "Lock, Stock and Two Smoking Barrels," "Snatch," and "Sherlock Holmes." I often collaborate with actors Jason Statham and Jude Law.

Who am I?

15. I am an Italian director celebrated for my epic historical dramas and sweeping visuals. My notable films include "The Leopard," "Death in Venice," and "Ludwig." My meticulous attention to detail has earned me critical acclaim.

Who am I?

Round 4: Expert

16. I am an Austrian-American filmmaker known for my pioneering work in the film noir genre. My famous films include "Double Indemnity," "Sunset Boulevard," and "Some Like It Hot." My sharp wit and satirical style are hallmarks of my work.

Who am I?

17. I am a Swedish director acclaimed for my profound exploration of existential themes. My notable works include "The Seventh Seal," "Wild Strawberries," and "Persona." My films often feature a stark and contemplative visual style.

Who am I?

18. I am an Italian filmmaker renowned for my surreal and autobiographical films. My famous works include "8½," "La Dolce Vita," and "Amarcord." My imaginative and visually extravagant style has influenced countless directors.

Who am I?

19. I am a Chinese director known for my visually stunning and emotionally powerful films. My famous works include "Raise the Red Lantern," "Hero," and "House of Flying Daggers." My use of color and composition is highly regarded.

Who am I?

20. I am a Russian filmmaker celebrated for my philosophical and visually poetic films. My notable works include "Andrei Rublev," "Solaris," and "Stalker." My contemplative and slow-paced style has left a lasting legacy in cinema.

Who am I?

Answers: Who Am I? - Famous Directors

1. Alfred Hitchcock

Did you know? Alfred Hitchcock originally wanted Cary Grant to play the role of Norman Bates in "Psycho," but the role ultimately went to Anthony Perkins.

2. Steven Spielberg

Did you know? Steven Spielberg was rejected from the University of Southern California's film school twice before eventually attending California State University, Long Beach.

3. Martin Scorsese

Did you know? Martin Scorsese has been nominated for the Academy Award for Best Director nine times but won only once for "The Departed."

4. John Carpenter

Did you know? John Carpenter's film "The Thing" was initially a box office failure but later gained a cult following and is now considered a classic.

5. Peter Jackson

Did you know? Peter Jackson made cameo appearances in all three of his "Lord of the Rings" films, including as a carrot-chomping citizen in "The Fellowship of the Ring."

6. Akira Kurosawa

Did you know? Akira Kurosawa's film "Rashomon" introduced the Western world to Japanese cinema and won the Golden Lion at the Venice Film Festival in 1951.

7. Tim Burton

Did you know? Tim Burton's first full-length film was "Pee-wee's Big Adventure," which was a surprise hit and launched his directorial career.

8. Ang Lee

Did you know? Ang Lee's "Life of Pi" won four Academy Awards, including Best Director, and is known for its groundbreaking visual effects.

9. Christopher Nolan

Did you know? Christopher Nolan often casts Michael Caine in his films, starting with "Batman Begins" and continuing through to "Tenet."

10. Charlie Chaplin

Did you know? Charlie Chaplin was knighted by Queen Elizabeth II in 1975, just two years before his death.

11. Jean-Luc Godard

Did you know? Jean-Luc Godard once used an actual gunshot sound instead of a traditional film clapboard to mark the start of scenes in "Breathless."

12. Guillermo del Toro

Did you know? Guillermo del Toro owns a house called "Bleak House," where he keeps his extensive collection of books, art, and film memorabilia.

13. Abbas Kiarostami

Did you know? Abbas Kiarostami's "Taste of Cherry" won the Palme d'Or at the Cannes Film Festival in 1997, despite its minimalist approach and ambiguous ending.

14. Guy Ritchie

Did you know? Guy Ritchie is an accomplished martial artist and holds a black belt in Brazilian Jiu-Jitsu.

15. Luchino Visconti

Did you know? Luchino Visconti was also an opera director and brought his theatrical experience to his visually grand films.

16. Billy Wilder

Did you know? Billy Wilder's "Some Like It Hot" was voted the greatest American comedy of all time by the American Film Institute.

17. Ingmar Bergman

Did you know? Ingmar Bergman wrote and directed more than 60 films and 170 plays, many of which explored themes of death, faith, and human relationships.

18. Federico Fellini

Did you know? Federico Fellini coined the term "paparazzi" from a character named Paparazzo in his film "La Dolce Vita."

19. Zhang Yimou

Did you know? Zhang Yimou directed the opening and closing ceremonies of the 2008 Beijing Olympics, which were praised for their artistic and technical excellence.

20. Andrei Tarkovsky

Did you know? Andrei Tarkovsky's film "Stalker" is rumored to have caused long-term health issues for the cast and crew due to the toxic locations where it was filmed.

Who Am I?

American Presidents

Round 1: Easy

1. I was the first President of the United States, serving from 1789 to 1797. Known as the "Father of His Country," I led the American Revolutionary War to victory against the British. I never lived in the White House as it wasn't completed during my presidency.

Who am I?

2. I was the principal author of the Declaration of Independence and the third President of the United States. My tenure saw the Louisiana Purchase, which doubled the size of the country. I kept a mockingbird named "Dick" as a pet.

Who am I?

3. I was the seventh President of the United States and am known for my strong populist views and leadership during the Indian Removal Act. I also fought in over 100 duels, defending my honor and often coming out unscathed.

Who am I?

4. I was the 16th President of the United States, leading the country through the Civil War. My leadership was instrumental in preserving the Union and abolishing slavery. I stored important documents, including the Gettysburg Address, in my iconic top hat.

Who am I?

5. I was the 26th President of the United States and a leader of the Progressive movement. Known for my exuberant personality and

cowboy persona, I delivered a 90-minute speech after being shot in the chest, with the bullet lodged in my rib.

Who am I?

Round 2: Medium

6. I was the 32nd President of the United States, serving four terms and leading the nation through the Great Depression and World War II. I used a wheelchair due to polio, but many Americans were unaware of my condition during my presidency.

Who am I?

7. I was the 34th President of the United States and a five-star general during World War II. I led the Allied forces in Europe and was instrumental in planning the D-Day invasion. I was also an avid golfer and even installed a putting green on the White House lawn.

Who am I?

8. I was the 35th President of the United States, known for my youthful charisma and ambitious vision. My administration navigated Cold War tensions, including the Cuban Missile Crisis. I had a well-documented love for sailing and spent many weekends on my yacht.

Who am I?

9. I was the 40th President of the United States and a former Hollywood actor. My presidency saw the end of the Cold War and the implementation of economic policies known as "Reaganomics." I loved horseback riding and frequently retreated to my ranch in California.

Who am I?

10. I was the 44th President of the United States and the first African American to hold the office. My leadership saw the enactment of significant healthcare reform. I once won a Grammy Award for Best Spoken Word Album for the audio version of my memoir.

Who am I?

Round 3: Hard

11. I was the 6th President of the United States and the son of a former president. I famously swam nude in the Potomac River every morning and later served as a congressman for 17 years after my presidency.

Who am I?

12. I was the 11th President of the United States and oversaw the Mexican-American War, which significantly expanded U.S. territory. I worked so diligently that I often slept in my office to ensure I was always ready to handle any crisis.

Who am I?

13. I was the 17th President of the United States and succeeded Abraham Lincoln after his assassination. My presidency was marked by clashes with Congress over Reconstruction policies. I apprenticed as a tailor in my youth and continued making clothes throughout my life.

Who am I?

14. I was the 21st President of the United States, ascending to the role after the assassination of James Garfield. I was known for my fashion sense and owned over 80 pairs of pants, earning me the nickname "Elegant Arthur."

Who am I?

15. I was the 27th President of the United States and later became Chief Justice of the Supreme Court, the only person to have held both positions. I once got stuck in the White House bathtub and had a larger one installed to accommodate my size.

Who am I?

Round 4: Expert

16. I was the 10th President of the United States and the first to assume the presidency due to the death of my predecessor. I fathered 15

children, the most of any president, and two of my grandsons are still alive today, despite my presidency being in the 1840s.

Who am I?

17. I was the 23rd President of the United States and the grandson of a former president. My term saw the admission of six new states to the Union. I installed electricity in the White House but was so afraid of getting shocked that I refused to touch the light switches.

Who am I?

18. I was the 30th President of the United States and known for my quiet demeanor, earning the nickname "Silent Cal." I enjoyed practical jokes and once bet a guest that he could make him say more than two words. The guest failed when I replied, "You lose."

Who am I?

19. I was the 31st President of the United States, serving during the onset of the Great Depression. Before my presidency, I was a successful mining engineer and amassed significant wealth, much of which I donated to charitable causes.

Who am I?

20. I was the 39th President of the United States and have been deeply involved in humanitarian efforts since leaving office. I won the Nobel Peace Prize in 2002. I am also known for my skills in carpentry and have helped build homes for Habitat for Humanity.

Who am I?

Answers: Who Am I? - American Presidents

1. George Washington

Did you know? George Washington was unanimously elected as the first president by the Electoral College and declined a third term, establishing a tradition of a peaceful transfer of power.

2. Thomas Jefferson

Did you know? Thomas Jefferson was an accomplished architect and designed his own estate, Monticello, as well as the buildings for the University of Virginia.

3. Andrew Jackson

Did you know? Andrew Jackson is featured on the $20 bill, despite his opposition to paper money and central banking.

4. Abraham Lincoln

Did you know? Abraham Lincoln is enshrined in the Wrestling Hall of Fame. He lost only one match out of 300 in his wrestling career.

5. Theodore Roosevelt

Did you know? Theodore Roosevelt was an avid naturalist and helped establish the National Park Service to preserve America's natural beauty.

6. Franklin D. Roosevelt

Did you know? Franklin D. Roosevelt is the only U.S. president to have served more than two terms, leading the country through some of its most challenging times.

7. Dwight D. Eisenhower

Did you know? Dwight D. Eisenhower was also the first president of all 50 states, as Alaska and Hawaii joined the Union during his administration.

8. John F. Kennedy

Did you know? John F. Kennedy was awarded the Pulitzer Prize for his book "Profiles in Courage," which profiles acts of bravery and integrity by eight U.S. Senators.

9. Ronald Reagan

Did you know? Ronald Reagan was also known for his love of jelly beans and always kept a jar of them in the Oval Office.

10. Barack Obama

Did you know? Barack Obama won the Nobel Peace Prize in 2009 for his efforts to strengthen international diplomacy and cooperation between peoples.

11. John Quincy Adams

Did you know? John Quincy Adams kept a pet alligator in the White House, a gift from the Marquis de Lafayette.

12. James K. Polk

Did you know? James K. Polk is often referred to as the "hardest working president" due to his intense work ethic and rigorous schedule.

13. Andrew Johnson

Did you know? Andrew Johnson is the only president to have served in the U.S. Senate after his presidency.

14. Chester A. Arthur

Did you know? Chester A. Arthur remodeled the White House extensively, including the installation of an elevator.

15. William Howard Taft

Did you know? William Howard Taft later served as Chief Justice of the Supreme Court, the only person to have held both positions.

16. John Tyler

Did you know? John Tyler's grandsons, Lyon Gardiner Tyler Jr. and Harrison Ruffin Tyler, were still alive as of 2020.

17. Benjamin Harrison

Did you know? Benjamin Harrison had a pet goat named Whiskers that roamed the White House grounds.

18. Calvin Coolidge

Did you know? Calvin Coolidge's pet raccoon, Rebecca, was given to him for Thanksgiving dinner, but he decided to keep her as a pet instead.

19. Herbert Hoover

Did you know? Herbert Hoover and his wife spoke fluent Mandarin Chinese and would converse in it to keep their conversations private.

20. Jimmy Carter

Did you know? Jimmy Carter has written over 30 books, including memoirs, poetry, and even a novel.

Who Am I?

American Singers

Round 1: Easy

1. I am known as the "King of Rock and Roll" and became a cultural icon in the 1950s. My famous hits include "Hound Dog," "Jailhouse Rock," and "Can't Help Falling in Love." I also had a fondness for peanut butter and banana sandwiches.

Who am I?

2. I was a pop sensation in the late 1990s and early 2000s with hits like "...Baby One More Time," "Oops!... I Did It Again," and "Toxic." I started my career on the Mickey Mouse Club.

Who am I?

3. I am a legendary singer and songwriter known for my powerful voice and hits like "Respect," "Natural Woman," and "Chain of Fools." I was crowned the "Queen of Soul."

Who am I?

4. I am a country music star known for my deep voice and hits like "I Walk the Line," "Ring of Fire," and "Folsom Prison Blues." I often wore black on stage, earning me the nickname "The Man in Black."

Who am I?

5. I am a pop icon who gained fame with my group Destiny's Child before launching a successful solo career. My hits include "Crazy in Love," "Single Ladies," and "Halo." I am married to rapper Jay-Z.

Who am I?

Round 2: Medium

6. I am a legendary jazz singer with a career spanning over 60 years. My famous songs include "Summertime," "Someone to Watch Over Me," and "Porgy and Bess." My nickname is "Lady Day."

Who am I?

7. I am a rock singer and songwriter known for my energetic performances and hits like "Born to Run," "Dancing in the Dark," and "Born in the U.S.A." I am often referred to as "The Boss."

Who am I?

8. I am a pop star who rose to fame with my album "1989" and hits like "Shake It Off," "Blank Space," and "Love Story." I started my career in country music before transitioning to pop.

Who am I?

9. I am a soul and R&B legend known for my smooth voice and hits like "Superstition," "Isn't She Lovely," and "I Just Called to Say I Love You." I was blind from birth and learned to play multiple instruments.

Who am I?

10. I am a hip-hop artist and producer known for my influential work in the genre. My hits include "Gold Digger," "Stronger," and "Heartless." I am also known for my outspoken personality and fashion ventures.

Who am I?

Round 3: Hard

11. I am an influential folk singer known for my poetic lyrics and songs like "Blowin' in the Wind," "The Times They Are A-Changin'," and "Like a Rolling Stone." I won the Nobel Prize in Literature in 2016.

Who am I?

12. I am a legendary blues singer and guitarist known for my distinctive voice and songs like "The Thrill Is Gone," "Every Day I Have the Blues," and "Lucille." My guitar is also named Lucille.

Who am I?

13. I am a groundbreaking pop and R&B singer known for my powerful voice and hits like "I Will Always Love You," "Greatest Love of All," and "I Wanna Dance with Somebody." I starred in the film "The Bodyguard."

Who am I?

14. I am a pioneering rock and roll artist known for my energetic piano playing and hits like "Tutti Frutti," "Long Tall Sally," and "Good Golly Miss Molly." My flamboyant style and stage presence were revolutionary.

Who am I?

15. I am an iconic singer-songwriter known for my introspective lyrics and hits like "Fire and Rain," "You've Got a Friend," and "Carolina in My Mind." I battled addiction early in my career and became a leading voice in the singer-songwriter movement.

Who am I?

Round 4: Expert

16. I am a legendary jazz trumpeter and singer known for my gravelly voice and songs like "What a Wonderful World," "Hello, Dolly!" and "La Vie En Rose." My nickname is "Satchmo."

Who am I?

17. I am a renowned soul singer known for my emotive voice and songs like "A Change Is Gonna Come," "Cupid," and "Twistin' the Night Away." My life was tragically cut short at the age of 33.

Who am I?

18. I am a pioneering country singer known for my distinctive voice and hits like "Crazy," "I Fall to Pieces," and "Walkin' After Midnight." I died in a plane crash at the age of 30.

Who am I?

19. I am an influential rock singer and songwriter known for my theatrical performances and hits like "Purple Rain," "When Doves Cry," and "Little Red Corvette." I was a multi-instrumentalist known for my eclectic style.

Who am I?

20. I am an iconic folk and country singer known for my soothing voice and hits like "Take Me Home, Country Roads," "Annie's Song," and "Rocky Mountain High." I died in a plane crash in 1997.

Who am I?

Answers: Who Am I? - American Singers

1. **Elvis Presley**

Did you know? Elvis Presley held a black belt in karate and often practiced martial arts both on and off stage.

2. **Britney Spears**

Did you know? Britney Spears once hosted "Saturday Night Live" and performed as both the host and musical guest.

3. **Aretha Franklin**

Did you know? Aretha Franklin performed at three presidential inaugurations: for Jimmy Carter, Bill Clinton, and Barack Obama.

4. Johnny Cash

Did you know? Johnny Cash wrote a novel called "Man in White" about the apostle Paul, reflecting his deep interest in religion.

5. Beyoncé

Did you know? Beyoncé was the first female artist to debut at number one on the Billboard 200 with her first five studio albums.

6. Billie Holiday

Did you know? Billie Holiday's song "Strange Fruit," a haunting protest against lynching, was inducted into the Grammy Hall of Fame in 1978.

7. Bruce Springsteen

Did you know? Bruce Springsteen was once mistaken for a homeless man and given spare change while walking in New York City.

8. Taylor Swift

Did you know? Taylor Swift has a framed photo of Kanye West interrupting her at the 2009 VMAs in her Nashville home, as a humorous reminder of the event.

9. Stevie Wonder

Did you know? Stevie Wonder recorded his first hit single, "Fingertips," at the age of 12, becoming the youngest artist to top the Billboard Hot 100.

10. Kanye West

Did you know? Kanye West's "My Beautiful Dark Twisted Fantasy" received a perfect score from numerous music critics and is considered one of the greatest albums of all time.

11. Bob Dylan

Did you know? Bob Dylan's real name is Robert Zimmerman, and he took his stage name from the poet Dylan Thomas.

12. B.B. King

Did you know? B.B. King performed over 200 concerts a year well into his 70s, showing his relentless passion for music.

13. Whitney Houston

Did you know? Whitney Houston's rendition of "The Star-Spangled Banner" at the 1991 Super Bowl became a best-selling single and was re-released after the 9/11 attacks.

14. Little Richard

Did you know? Little Richard's flamboyant persona and stage presence influenced future rock stars like Prince, David Bowie, and Elton John.

15. James Taylor

Did you know? James Taylor was once signed to The Beatles' Apple Records and released his debut album under their label.

16. Louis Armstrong

Did you know? Louis Armstrong's distinctive voice and trumpet playing made him one of the first African-American entertainers to gain widespread popularity in the mainstream.

17. Sam Cooke

Did you know? Sam Cooke's posthumous influence includes artists like Otis Redding and Aretha Franklin, who both cited him as an inspiration.

18. Patsy Cline

Did you know? Patsy Cline's "Crazy" was written by Willie Nelson and is one of the most frequently played jukebox songs of all time.

19. Prince

Did you know? Prince changed his name to an unpronounceable symbol in the 1990s due to a contractual dispute with his record label.

20. John Denver

Did you know? John Denver was an avid environmentalist and founded the Windstar Foundation to promote sustainable living.

Who Am I?

British/Irish Singers

Round 1: Easy

1. I was the lead vocalist of the legendary British rock band Queen. Known for my flamboyant stage presence and powerful voice, my hits include "Bohemian Rhapsody," "We Will Rock You," and "Somebody to Love."

Who am I?

2. I am a British singer-songwriter known for my soul and jazz-influenced music. My breakout album "Back to Black" won five Grammy Awards, and my hit songs include "Rehab" and "Valerie."

Who am I?

3. I was the lead singer of the British band The Beatles and later had a successful solo career. My famous songs include "Imagine," "Hey Jude," and "Let It Be."

Who am I?

4. I am a British singer and actor who was part of the boy band One Direction before launching a successful solo career. My hits include "Sign of the Times" and "Watermelon Sugar."

Who am I?

5. I am an Irish singer known for my unique voice and as the frontman of the rock band U2. My famous songs include "With or Without You," "One," and "Beautiful Day."

Who am I?

Round 2: Medium

6. I am a British singer-songwriter known for my hit songs "Shape of You," "Thinking Out Loud," and "Perfect." I often perform with just a guitar and a loop pedal.

Who am I?

7. I am a British singer and guitarist who was a member of the band Oasis. My famous songs include "Wonderwall," "Don't Look Back in Anger," and "Live Forever."

Who am I?

8. I am an English singer known for my powerful voice and hits like "Rolling in the Deep," "Someone Like You," and "Hello." My album "21" became one of the best-selling albums of the 21st century.

Who am I?

9. I was the lead singer of the Irish rock band The Cranberries. My distinctive voice was featured in hits like "Linger," "Zombie," and "Dreams."

Who am I?

10. I am a British singer known for my operatic pop style and hits like "Time to Say Goodbye" (with Andrea Bocelli) and "Deliver Me." I also performed at the 2012 London Olympics opening ceremony.

Who am I?

Round 3: Hard

11. I am a British singer-songwriter and guitarist known for my work with the band The Police and my solo career. My famous songs include "Roxanne," "Every Breath You Take," and "Fields of Gold."

Who am I?

12. I am a British singer and pianist known for my elaborate stage costumes and numerous hit songs. My famous songs include "Rocket Man," "Tiny Dancer," and "Your Song."

Who am I?

13. I am an English singer and member of the band The Rolling Stones. My energetic performances and distinctive voice have made me an enduring rock icon. My famous songs include "Satisfaction," "Paint It Black," and "Angie."

Who am I?

14. I am a British singer known for my deep voice and dramatic ballads. My famous songs include "Love Me Tender," "Delilah," and "It's Not Unusual." I was also a judge on "The Voice UK."

Who am I?

15. I am an Irish singer-songwriter known for my protest songs and distinctive voice. My famous works include "Nothing Compares 2 U" and "The Emperor's New Clothes."

Who am I?

Round 4: Expert

16. I am a British singer and songwriter known for my eclectic style and the hit "Space Oddity." My constant reinvention of my music and image made me one of the most influential musicians of the 20th century.

Who am I?

17. I am a British singer known for my haunting voice and gothic appearance. My famous songs include "Wuthering Heights," "Running Up That Hill," and "Babooshka."

Who am I?

18. I am an Irish singer and guitarist who was a founding member of the band Thin Lizzy. My famous songs include "The Boys Are Back in Town" and "Whiskey in the Jar."

Who am I?

19. I am a British singer and songwriter known for my innovative music and influence on punk rock. My famous songs include "London Calling," "Should I Stay or Should I Go," and "Rock the Casbah."

Who am I?

20. I am a British singer known for my androgynous style and new wave hits. My famous songs include "Karma Chameleon" and "Do You Really Want to Hurt Me."

Who am I?

Answers: Who Am I? - British/Irish Singers

1. Freddie Mercury

Did you know? Freddie Mercury designed the Queen emblem, incorporating the zodiac signs of all the band members.

2. Amy Winehouse

Did you know? Amy Winehouse was posthumously awarded the Grammy Award for Best Pop Duo/Group Performance for her duet with Tony Bennett, "Body and Soul."

3. John Lennon

Did you know? John Lennon's middle name was Winston, after Winston Churchill, though he later changed it to Ono after marrying Yoko Ono.

4. Harry Styles

Did you know? Harry Styles became the first man to appear solo on the cover of Vogue magazine in 2020.

5. Bono

Did you know? Bono's real name is Paul David Hewson, and his stage name was inspired by a hearing aid shop called Bono Vox, which means "good voice."

6. Ed Sheeran

Did you know? Ed Sheeran appeared as a Lannister soldier in an episode of "Game of Thrones."

7. Noel Gallagher

Did you know? Noel Gallagher's brother, Liam Gallagher, was the lead vocalist of Oasis, and their sibling rivalry was legendary in the music industry.

8. Adele

Did you know? Adele's album "25" was the best-selling album worldwide for both 2015 and 2016.

9. Dolores O'Riordan

Did you know? Dolores O'Riordan once bought a medieval castle in Ireland and lived there with her family.

10. Sarah Brightman

Did you know? Sarah Brightman was originally cast in the role of Jemima in the original London production of "Cats."

11. Sting

Did you know? Sting's real name is Gordon Sumner, and he got his nickname from a black and yellow striped sweater he used to wear, which made him look like a bee.

12. Elton John

Did you know? Elton John was knighted by Queen Elizabeth II in 1998 for his services to music and charitable services.

13. Mick Jagger

Did you know? Mick Jagger studied at the London School of Economics before dedicating himself to a career in music.

14. Tom Jones

Did you know? Tom Jones received a knighthood from Queen Elizabeth II in 2006 for his services to music.

15. Sinéad O'Connor

Did you know? Sinéad O'Connor caused a major controversy by tearing up a photo of Pope John Paul II on live television during a performance on "Saturday Night Live."

16. David Bowie

Did you know? David Bowie's real name was David Robert Jones, but he changed it to avoid confusion with Davy Jones of The Monkees.

17. Kate Bush

Did you know? Kate Bush wrote her hit song "Wuthering Heights" when she was just 18 years old, inspired by Emily Brontë's novel of the same name.

18. Phil Lynott

Did you know? Phil Lynott was the first black Irishman to achieve commercial success in the field of rock music.

19. Joe Strummer

Did you know? Joe Strummer's real name was John Mellor, and he was born in Ankara, Turkey, to a British diplomat.

20. Boy George

Did you know? Boy George, born George Alan O'Dowd, is also a successful DJ and fashion designer.

Who Am I?

Cold War Figures

Round 1: Easy

1. I was the 35th President of the United States, serving from 1961 until my assassination in 1963. My administration navigated the Cuban Missile Crisis and I delivered the famous "Ich bin ein Berliner" speech.

Who am I?

2. I was the leader of the Soviet Union from 1953 to 1964, known for my de-Stalinization policies and the famous kitchen debate with Richard Nixon. I also presided over the Cuban Missile Crisis from the Soviet side.

Who am I?

3. I was the British Prime Minister known for my "Iron Curtain" speech, delivered in 1946. I led Britain during World War II and returned to office during the early years of the Cold War.

Who am I?

4. I was the 40th President of the United States, serving from 1981 to 1989. My policies contributed to the end of the Cold War, and I famously demanded, "Mr. Gorbachev, tear down this wall!"

Who am I?

5. I was the leader of the Soviet Union from 1985 until its dissolution in 1991. My policies of glasnost and perestroika aimed to reform the Communist Party and the Soviet state.

Who am I?

Round 2: Medium

6. I was the Secretary of State under Presidents Nixon and Ford, playing a crucial role in the policy of détente and the opening of diplomatic relations with China. I won the Nobel Peace Prize in 1973.

Who am I?

7. I was the East German leader from 1971 to 1989, known for my staunch support of the Berlin Wall and alignment with Soviet policies. My regime fell just before the wall was dismantled.

Who am I?

8. I was the General Secretary of the Communist Party of China from 1949 until my death in 1976. I was the founding father of the People's Republic of China and a key figure during the Korean War.

Who am I?

9. I was the architect of the American containment strategy during the Cold War, serving as a diplomat and historian. My "Long Telegram" outlined the need to contain Soviet expansion.

Who am I?

10. I was the leader of Cuba from 1959 until my retirement in 2008. My alliance with the Soviet Union brought the world to the brink of nuclear war during the Cuban Missile Crisis.

Who am I?

Round 3: Hard

11. I was the West German Chancellor who played a significant role in the rapprochement between East and West Germany, winning the Nobel Peace Prize in 1971 for my efforts in Ostpolitik.

Who am I?

12. I was the Soviet Premier known for initiating the invasion of Afghanistan in 1979, a decision that significantly strained US-Soviet relations and led to a decade-long conflict.

Who am I?

13. I was a prominent American senator known for my anti-Communist crusades in the early 1950s, which led to a period of intense suspicion and fear known as the Red Scare.

Who am I?

14. I was the first President of the Fifth Republic of France and a key figure in establishing France's independent nuclear deterrent and withdrawing from NATO's military command.

Who am I?

15. I was the Yugoslav leader who resisted Soviet control and founded the Non-Aligned Movement, maintaining a neutral stance during the Cold War.

Who am I?

Answers: Who Am I? - Cold War Figures

1. John F. Kennedy

Did you know? John F. Kennedy's presidency saw the establishment of the Peace Corps and the start of the Apollo space program.

2. Nikita Khrushchev

Did you know? Nikita Khrushchev once famously banged his shoe on the podium during a speech at the United Nations General Assembly.

3. Winston Churchill

Did you know? Winston Churchill won the Nobel Prize in Literature in 1953 for his numerous published works, especially his six-volume series "The Second World War."

4. Ronald Reagan

Did you know? Ronald Reagan was an actor before entering politics, starring in over 50 films and television series.

5. Mikhail Gorbachev

Did you know? Mikhail Gorbachev won the Nobel Peace Prize in 1990 for his role in ending the Cold War.

6. Henry Kissinger

Did you know? Henry Kissinger was born in Germany and emigrated to the United States in 1938 to escape Nazi persecution.

7. Erich Honecker

Did you know? Erich Honecker was ousted from power just weeks before the fall of the Berlin Wall in 1989.

8. Mao Zedong

Did you know? Mao Zedong's Cultural Revolution led to significant upheaval and the persecution of millions of people in China.

9. George F. Kennan

Did you know? George F. Kennan's "X Article" in Foreign Affairs magazine in 1947 laid out the principles of containment that shaped US Cold War policy.

10. Fidel Castro

Did you know? Fidel Castro survived numerous assassination attempts by the CIA, including plots involving exploding cigars and poisoned diving suits.

11. Willy Brandt

Did you know? Willy Brandt fled Nazi Germany and worked as a journalist in Norway before returning to Germany after World War II to pursue a political career.

12. Leonid Brezhnev

Did you know? Leonid Brezhnev was known for his heavy military spending and his era of stagnation in the Soviet Union's economy.

13. Joseph McCarthy

Did you know? Joseph McCarthy's aggressive investigations and accusations led to the coining of the term "McCarthyism," synonymous with witch hunts and unfounded accusations.

14. Charles de Gaulle

Did you know? Charles de Gaulle's policy of "grandeur" aimed to elevate France's global standing, leading to the development of an independent nuclear force.

15. Josip Broz Tito

Did you know? Josip Broz Tito managed to keep Yugoslavia independent from Soviet influence, creating a unique form of socialism known as Titoism.

Who Am I?

Famous Kings and Queens

Round 1: Easy

1. I was the Queen of England from 1558 to 1603, known as the "Virgin Queen." My reign saw the defeat of the Spanish Armada and the flourishing of English drama, including the works of Shakespeare.

Who am I?

2. I was the King of France from 1643 to 1715, known as the "Sun King." My reign is the longest recorded of any monarch of a sovereign country in European history, and I built the Palace of Versailles.

Who am I?

3. I am the current Queen of the United Kingdom, having ascended the throne in 1952. My reign has seen significant changes in the British Empire and society, and I celebrated my Platinum Jubilee in 2022.

Who am I?

4. I was the first Emperor of China, known for unifying the country and starting the construction of the Great Wall. My tomb is guarded by the famous Terracotta Army.

Who am I?

5. I was the Queen of Ancient Egypt and one of the most famous female pharaohs. My romantic liaisons with Julius Caesar and Mark Antony have been the subject of many historical and fictional works.

Who am I?

Round 2: Medium

6. I was the King of Macedonia who created one of the largest empires in history by the age of 30. My conquests spread Greek culture throughout the known world and I was tutored by Aristotle.

Who am I?

7. I was the King of England from 1189 to 1199, known for my role in the Third Crusade and my epithet "Lionheart." I spent very little time in England during my reign.

Who am I?

8. I was the Empress of Russia from 1762 to 1796, known for my ambitious expansionist policies and efforts to modernize Russia. My reign is often referred to as the Golden Age of the Russian Empire.

Who am I?

9. I was the Queen of Scots from 1542 to 1567, executed by my cousin Elizabeth I of England. My life was marked by a series of dramatic events, including multiple marriages and imprisonments.

Who am I?

10. I was the King of the Franks and Lombards before being crowned Emperor of the Romans in 800 AD, reviving the title of Emperor in Western Europe. I am often referred to as the "Father of Europe."

Who am I?

Round 3: Hard

11. I was the Queen of Castile and León from 1474 to 1504, who financed Christopher Columbus's 1492 voyage to the New World. My marriage to Ferdinand II of Aragon helped unify Spain.

Who am I?

12. I was the King of the United Kingdom who abdicated the throne in 1936 to marry Wallis Simpson, an American divorcee. My abdication led to a constitutional crisis and my brother becoming king.

Who am I?

13. I was the last Tsar of Russia, ruling from 1894 until my abdication in 1917. My reign ended with the Russian Revolution, and my family and I were executed by the Bolsheviks.

Who am I?

14. I was the Queen of the British Iceni tribe who led an uprising against the occupying Roman forces in 60/61 AD. My revolt is one of the most famous events in Roman Britain.

Who am I?

15. I was the King of Prussia from 1740 to 1786, known for my military victories, patronage of the arts, and enlightenment ideals. My reign greatly expanded Prussian territories.

Who am I?

Answers: Who Am I? - Famous Kings and Queens

1. Queen Elizabeth I

Did you know? Queen Elizabeth I never married and was known for her elaborate and colorful clothing, which symbolized the wealth and power of her reign.

2. King Louis XIV

Did you know? King Louis XIV was an accomplished dancer and often performed in ballets at his court.

3. Queen Elizabeth II

Did you know? Queen Elizabeth II has owned more than 30 corgis during her reign and is known for her love of dogs.

4. Qin Shi Huang

Did you know? Qin Shi Huang's mausoleum, which houses the Terracotta Army, was discovered in 1974 by local farmers in Shaanxi province.

5. Cleopatra VII

Did you know? Cleopatra VII could speak multiple languages, including Egyptian, Greek, and Latin.

6. Alexander the Great

Did you know? Alexander the Great never lost a battle and named over 70 cities after himself, the most famous being Alexandria in Egypt.

7. Richard the Lionheart

Did you know? Richard the Lionheart was captured and held for ransom by the Holy Roman Emperor Henry VI, and his release cost England a vast amount of money.

8. Catherine the Great

Did you know? Catherine the Great corresponded with many Enlightenment thinkers, including Voltaire and Diderot.

9. Mary, Queen of Scots

Did you know? Mary, Queen of Scots, was only six days old when she became queen after her father died.

10. Charlemagne

Did you know? Charlemagne's empire covered much of Western Europe, and he was a key figure in the Carolingian Renaissance, a revival of art, culture, and learning.

11. Queen Isabella I

Did you know? Queen Isabella I also established the Spanish Inquisition to maintain Catholic orthodoxy in her kingdoms.

12. King Edward VIII

Did you know? King Edward VIII was given the title Duke of Windsor after his abdication and spent most of his remaining life in France.

13. Tsar Nicholas II

Did you know? Tsar Nicholas II was the first cousin of King George V of England and Kaiser Wilhelm II of Germany.

14. Boudica

Did you know? Boudica's forces destroyed the Roman cities of Camulodunum (Colchester), Londinium (London), and Verulamium (St Albans) during her revolt.

15. Frederick the Great

Did you know? Frederick the Great was also a talented musician and composer, playing the flute and writing many pieces of music.

Who Am I?

Famous Scientists

Round 1: Easy

1. I developed the theory of relativity, and my equation $E=mc^2$ is one of the most famous in the world. I won the Nobel Prize in Physics in 1921.

Who am I?

2. I formulated the laws of motion and universal gravitation. My book, "Principia Mathematica," is considered one of the most important works in the history of science.

Who am I?

3. I am known as the father of modern physics and made significant improvements to the telescope. My support for heliocentrism led to conflicts with the Catholic Church.

Who am I?

4. I discovered the law of inheritance and established the principles of heredity using pea plants. I am often referred to as the father of genetics.

Who am I?

5. I developed the polio vaccine, which has saved millions of lives worldwide. I chose not to patent it, making it widely accessible.

Who am I?

Round 2: Medium

6. I discovered the structure of DNA along with James Watson and Maurice Wilkins. We shared the Nobel Prize in Physiology or Medicine in 1962.

Who am I?

7. I am the father of modern chemistry and developed the law of conservation of mass. I also identified and named oxygen and hydrogen.

Who am I?

8. I discovered penicillin, the first true antibiotic, which has saved countless lives since its introduction.

Who am I?

9. I am known for my laws of planetary motion, which describe the orbits of planets around the sun. My work provided the foundation for Newton's theory of gravitation.

Who am I?

10. I am a theoretical physicist known for my work on black holes and the author of "A Brief History of Time." Despite being diagnosed with ALS, I made significant contributions to cosmology.

Who am I?

Round 3: Hard

11. I am a pioneering physicist and chemist who discovered radioactivity and won Nobel Prizes in both Physics and Chemistry. My discoveries include polonium and radium.

Who am I?

12. I am known as the father of microbiology and developed the germ theory of disease. My work led to the development of vaccines for rabies and anthrax.

Who am I?

13. I developed the first successful human blood transfusion and introduced antiseptic surgical methods, greatly reducing infection rates.

Who am I?

14. I was the first woman to win a Nobel Prize, and I discovered the elements polonium and radium. My research was crucial in the development of X-ray machines.

Who am I?

15. I am known for my work on the electromagnetic theory of light and the equations that bear my name, which form the foundation of classical electromagnetism.

Who am I?

Round 4: Expert

16. I am the founder of the field of psychoanalysis and introduced concepts such as the unconscious mind, defense mechanisms, and dream interpretation.

Who am I?

17. I am a British naturalist who formulated the theory of evolution by natural selection, published in "On the Origin of Species."

Who am I?

18. I was a mathematician and logician who made significant contributions to computer science and artificial intelligence. The test that bears my name is a measure of a machine's ability to exhibit intelligent behavior.

Who am I?

19. I am known for my uncertainty principle in quantum mechanics, which states that the position and momentum of a particle cannot both be precisely determined at the same time.

Who am I?

20. I am an American physicist who was a key figure in the development of the atomic bomb during World War II, leading the Manhattan Project.

Who am I?

Answers: Who Am I? - Famous Scientists

1. **Albert Einstein**

Did you know? Albert Einstein was offered the presidency of Israel in 1952 but declined the offer.

2. Isaac Newton

Did you know? Isaac Newton also made significant contributions to optics and developed the first practical reflecting telescope.

3. Galileo Galilei

Did you know? Galileo's improvements to the telescope allowed him to make groundbreaking astronomical observations, including the moons of Jupiter.

4. Gregor Mendel

Did you know? Gregor Mendel's work on genetics was not widely recognized until after his death, long after he had published his findings.

5. Jonas Salk

Did you know? Jonas Salk's polio vaccine was first tested in 1952, and by 1955, it was declared safe and effective.

6. Francis Crick

Did you know? Francis Crick and James Watson famously used Rosalind Franklin's X-ray diffraction images of DNA to help determine its structure.

7. Antoine Lavoisier

Did you know? Antoine Lavoisier was executed by guillotine during the French Revolution, despite his significant contributions to science.

8. Alexander Fleming

Did you know? Alexander Fleming discovered penicillin by accident when he noticed that a mold called Penicillium notatum killed bacteria in a petri dish.

9. Johannes Kepler

Did you know? Johannes Kepler also worked as an assistant to the astronomer Tycho Brahe, whose precise observations helped Kepler develop his laws.

10. Stephen Hawking

Did you know? Stephen Hawking held the position of Lucasian Professor of Mathematics at the University of Cambridge, a position once held by Isaac Newton.

11. Marie Curie

Did you know? Marie Curie was the first person to win two Nobel Prizes in different scientific fields, Physics and Chemistry.

12. Louis Pasteur

Did you know? Louis Pasteur's process of pasteurization, which bears his name, is still used today to kill harmful bacteria in food and drinks.

13. James Blundell

Did you know? James Blundell performed the first successful transfusion of human blood in 1818, primarily to treat postpartum hemorrhage.

14. Marie Curie

Did you know? Marie Curie established mobile radiography units during World War I to assist in battlefield surgeries.

15. James Clerk Maxwell

Did you know? James Clerk Maxwell's work in electromagnetism paved the way for modern physics, including the theory of relativity and quantum mechanics.

16. Sigmund Freud

Did you know? Sigmund Freud's theories on the unconscious mind revolutionized the field of psychology, although many of his ideas are now considered controversial.

17. Charles Darwin

Did you know? Charles Darwin's voyage on the HMS Beagle provided him with the observations that led to his groundbreaking theory of natural selection.

18. Alan Turing

Did you know? Alan Turing's work on breaking the Enigma code during World War II significantly contributed to the Allied victory.

19. Werner Heisenberg

Did you know? Werner Heisenberg was awarded the Nobel Prize in Physics in 1932 for the creation of quantum mechanics.

20. J. Robert Oppenheimer

Did you know? J. Robert Oppenheimer later expressed deep remorse for his role in developing nuclear weapons, famously quoting the Bhagavad Gita: "Now I am become Death, the destroyer of worlds."

Who Am I?

Famous Actors

Round 1: Easy

1. I am known for my roles as a rugged archaeologist and a space smuggler. My famous lines include "It's not the years, honey, it's the mileage" and "I love you. I know."

Who am I?

2. I am an actor famous for my roles in "Titanic," "Inception," and "The Revenant." I finally won my first Oscar for playing a frontiersman left for dead in the wilderness.

Who am I?

3. I played a superhero in the Marvel Cinematic Universe, known for wielding a hammer and having a Norse mythology-inspired name. My character is the God of Thunder.

Who am I?

4. I starred as a high school chemistry teacher turned methamphetamine manufacturer in "Breaking Bad." My iconic line is "I am the one who knocks!"

Who am I?

5. I am known for my role as a pirate captain with a peculiar accent and love for rum. My character is constantly seeking the Black Pearl.

Who am I?

Round 2: Medium

6. I played a British secret agent with a license to kill, known for my suave demeanor and catchphrase "Shaken, not stirred." I recently concluded my tenure as this iconic character.

Who am I?

7. I am known for my roles in "Pretty Woman," "Erin Brockovich," and "Ocean's Eleven." I won an Oscar for portraying a legal assistant who helps win a major case against a power company.

Who am I?

8. I played a young wizard with a lightning bolt-shaped scar on his forehead. My journey involves fighting against the dark wizard Voldemort.

Who am I?

9. I am an Australian actor who played Wolverine in the X-Men series and also starred in "Les Misérables" and "The Greatest Showman."

Who am I?

10. I am famous for my comedic roles in "Ace Ventura: Pet Detective," "The Mask," and "Liar Liar." My expressive facial features and slapstick humor are my trademarks.

Who am I?

Round 3: Hard

11. I played a character who ages backward in "The Curious Case of Benjamin Button" and also starred in "Fight Club" and "Once Upon a Time in Hollywood."

Who am I?

12. I am an actor known for my roles in "Good Will Hunting," "The Bourne Identity," and "The Martian." I co-wrote and starred in a film that won an Oscar for Best Original Screenplay.

Who am I?

13. I am known for my role as a mathematician with schizophrenia in "A Beautiful Mind" and as a Roman general in "Gladiator." My famous line is "Are you not entertained?"

Who am I?

14. I played a boxer in "Rocky," a Vietnam War veteran in "First Blood," and a mercenary in "The Expendables." I am also known for my distinctive voice and muscular physique.

Who am I?

15. I starred as a quirky chocolatier in "Charlie and the Chocolate Factory" and as an eccentric Mad Hatter in "Alice in Wonderland." My collaborations with director Tim Burton are well-known.

Who am I?

Round 4: Expert

16. I am an actor known for my intense method acting and roles in "There Will Be Blood," "Gangs of New York," and "Lincoln." I have won three Oscars for Best Actor.

Who am I?

17. I am a Japanese actor famous for my collaborations with director Akira Kurosawa in films like "Seven Samurai," "Rashomon," and "Yojimbo." I am considered one of Japan's greatest actors.

Who am I?

18. I am known for my performances in "The Silence of the Lambs," "The Remains of the Day," and "Westworld." I often portray characters with complex and dark personalities.

Who am I?

19. I starred as an alcoholic country singer in "Walk the Line" and a mentally troubled man in "Joker." I am known for my intense and immersive acting style.

Who am I?

20. I am an Italian actor known for my work in spaghetti westerns, particularly in "The Good, the Bad and the Ugly." My iconic squint and tough-guy persona are unforgettable.

Who am I?

Answers: Who Am I? - Famous Actors

1. Harrison Ford

Did you know? Harrison Ford was a carpenter before becoming an actor, and he was discovered by George Lucas while building cabinets for the director.

2. Leonardo DiCaprio

Did you know? Leonardo DiCaprio's name was inspired by the artist Leonardo da Vinci because his pregnant mother felt him kick while looking at a da Vinci painting.

3. Chris Hemsworth

Did you know? Chris Hemsworth almost quit acting before landing his role as Thor due to a lack of steady work and considered becoming a builder.

4. Bryan Cranston

Did you know? Bryan Cranston once worked as a murder suspect on a cross-country motorcycle trip before becoming an actor, sparking his interest in crime stories.

5. Johnny Depp

Did you know? Johnny Depp is also a talented musician and has played guitar for bands like The Hollywood Vampires alongside Alice Cooper and Joe Perry.

6. Daniel Craig

Did you know? Daniel Craig performed many of his own stunts in his James Bond films, leading to several injuries over the years.

7. Julia Roberts

Did you know? Julia Roberts is the first actress to receive a $20 million paycheck for a single film, earning it for her role in "Erin Brockovich."

8. Daniel Radcliffe

Did you know? Daniel Radcliffe was cast as Harry Potter after the producer saw him in a theater production and recognized his potential for the role.

9. Hugh Jackman

Did you know? Hugh Jackman holds the Guinness World Record for the longest career as a live-action Marvel superhero, having played Wolverine for 17 years.

10. Jim Carrey

Did you know? Jim Carrey wrote himself a $10 million check for "acting services rendered" when he was a struggling actor, which he eventually cashed after becoming successful.

11. Brad Pitt

Did you know? Brad Pitt's breakout role in "Thelma & Louise" as a charming drifter earned him the status of a Hollywood heartthrob.

12. Matt Damon

Did you know? Matt Damon and Ben Affleck were childhood friends and co-wrote the screenplay for "Good Will Hunting" while living together in Los Angeles.

13. Russell Crowe

Did you know? Russell Crowe has a side career as a musician and leads the band 30 Odd Foot of Grunts, later renamed The Ordinary Fear of God.

14. Sylvester Stallone

Did you know? Sylvester Stallone wrote the screenplay for "Rocky" in just three days and insisted on starring in it, despite being an unknown actor at the time.

15. Johnny Depp

Did you know? Johnny Depp's character in "Pirates of the Caribbean" was inspired by Rolling Stones guitarist Keith Richards, who later played Depp's father in the film series.

16. Daniel Day-Lewis

Did you know? Daniel Day-Lewis is known for staying in character throughout the entire shooting process, even off-camera, to deliver authentic performances.

17. Toshiro Mifune

Did you know? Toshiro Mifune was discovered during an audition for Toho Studios' "New Face" contest, despite having no formal acting training.

18. Anthony Hopkins

Did you know? Anthony Hopkins memorized entire pages of scripts and sometimes the entire screenplay, even for scenes he wasn't in, to fully immerse himself in his roles.

19. Joaquin Phoenix

Did you know? Joaquin Phoenix received a standing ovation at the Venice Film Festival for his performance in "Joker," which won the Golden Lion award.

20. Clint Eastwood

Did you know? Clint Eastwood served as mayor of Carmel-by-the-Sea, California, from 1986 to 1988, and he owns the Mission Ranch Hotel and Restaurant in the town.

Who Are We?
American Bands

Round 1: Easy

1. We are a rock band known for our iconic "Hotel California," which features one of the most famous guitar solos in rock history. Our greatest hits album is one of the best-selling albums of all time.

Who are we?

2. We revolutionized the rock and roll scene in the 1960s with hits like "Good Vibrations" and "Surfin' USA." Our harmonies and beach-themed songs defined a generation.

Who are we?

3. We are a grunge band from Seattle that brought the genre to mainstream success with our album "Nevermind" and the iconic song "Smells Like Teen Spirit."

Who are we?

4. We are known for our genre-defining rap and hip-hop hits like "Fight For Your Right" and "Sabotage." We were pioneers in blending rock and hip-hop in the 1980s and 1990s.

Who are we?

5. We are a rock band from Boston famous for power ballads and arena anthems like "Dream On," "Sweet Emotion," and "Walk This Way," the latter of which we re-recorded with Run-DMC.

Who are we?

Round 2: Medium

6. We are a funk rock band known for hits like "Give It Away," "Californication," and "Under the Bridge." Our energetic performances and distinctive sound have made us one of the best-selling bands of all time.

Who are we?

7. We are a punk rock band from California that gained fame in the 1990s with hits like "Basket Case," "When I Come Around," and the rock opera "American Idiot."

Who are we?

8. We are a legendary heavy metal band known for our powerful anthems like "Enter Sandman," "Master of Puppets," and "Nothing Else Matters." Our aggressive sound and loyal fan base have kept us at the top for decades.

Who are we?

9. We are a southern rock band known for hits like "Sweet Home Alabama" and "Free Bird." Despite a tragic plane crash in 1977, our music remains iconic in rock history.

Who are we?

10. We are a hip-hop group from New York known for our groundbreaking album "Licensed to Ill" and later work that pushed the boundaries of hip-hop and rock fusion.

Who are we?

Round 3: Hard

11. We are an alternative rock band from San Francisco known for hits like "Semi-Charmed Life" and "Jumper." Our catchy melodies and reflective lyrics defined the late 1990s alternative scene.

Who are we?

12. We are a New York-based band known for our punk rock energy and hits like "Blitzkrieg Bop" and "I Wanna Be Sedated." Our leather jackets and fast-paced songs made us icons of punk rock.

Who are we?

13. We are an influential rock band from Georgia known for our eclectic sound and hits like "Losing My Religion" and "Everybody Hurts." Our music often explores themes of politics, spirituality, and human emotion.

Who are we?

14. We are a jazz-rock band from Chicago known for hits like "25 or 6 to 4" and "If You Leave Me Now." Our extensive use of brass instruments set us apart from many other rock bands.

Who are we?

15. We are a band from Los Angeles that brought rap rock to the mainstream with hits like "Killing in the Name" and "Bulls on Parade." Our politically charged lyrics and aggressive style have made us influential in both music and activism.

Who are we?

Answers: Who Are We? - American Bands

1. The Eagles

Did you know? The Eagles' "Their Greatest Hits (1971–1975)" is one of the best-selling albums in history, with over 38 million copies sold in the U.S. alone.

2. The Beach Boys

Did you know? The Beach Boys' album "Pet Sounds" is often cited as one of the greatest albums of all time and heavily influenced The Beatles' "Sgt. Pepper's Lonely Hearts Club Band."

3. Nirvana

Did you know? Nirvana's album "Nevermind" knocked Michael Jackson's "Dangerous" off the top of the Billboard charts in 1992.

4. Beastie Boys

Did you know? The Beastie Boys were the first rap group to top the Billboard 200 chart with their debut album "Licensed to Ill."

5. Aerosmith

Did you know? Aerosmith's collaboration with Run-DMC on "Walk This Way" helped break down racial barriers in the music industry and brought hip-hop to a wider audience.

6. Red Hot Chili Peppers

Did you know? Red Hot Chili Peppers hold the record for the most number-one singles (13) on the Billboard Alternative Songs chart.

7. Green Day

Did you know? Green Day's "American Idiot" was adapted into a successful Broadway musical that premiered in 2010.

8. Metallica

Did you know? Metallica's 1991 self-titled album, also known as "The Black Album," is one of the best-selling albums worldwide, with over 30 million copies sold.

9. Lynyrd Skynyrd

Did you know? Despite their Southern roots, Lynyrd Skynyrd's most famous song, "Sweet Home Alabama," was written in response to songs by Neil Young criticizing the South.

10. Beastie Boys

Did you know? The Beastie Boys' "Licensed to Ill" was the first rap album to reach number one on the Billboard 200 chart.

11. Third Eye Blind

Did you know? Third Eye Blind's debut album, released in 1997, went six times platinum and included five singles that charted on the Billboard Hot 100.

12. Ramones

Did you know? The Ramones' self-titled debut album is considered one of the greatest punk albums of all time and had a significant impact on the punk rock movement.

13. R.E.M.

Did you know? R.E.M. was one of the first alternative rock bands to achieve mainstream success, and they were inducted into the Rock and Roll Hall of Fame in 2007.

14. Chicago

Did you know? Chicago is one of the longest-running and best-selling music groups of all time, with over 100 million records sold worldwide.

15. Rage Against the Machine

Did you know? Rage Against the Machine's debut album is celebrated for its revolutionary political messages and has been included in Rolling Stone's list of the 500 greatest albums of all time.

Who Are We?

British and Irish Bands

Round 1: Easy

1. We are a British rock band known for our iconic albums "Sgt. Pepper's Lonely Hearts Club Band" and "Abbey Road." Our members included John, Paul, George, and Ringo. We also made a landmark animated film featuring a yellow submarine.

Who are we?

2. We are an Irish rock band famous for our anthems "With or Without You," "Beautiful Day," and "Sunday Bloody Sunday." Our lead singer is known as Bono, and we often perform against a backdrop of political and social activism.

Who are we?

3. We are a British rock band whose hit "Bohemian Rhapsody" has become a timeless classic. Our lead singer was the flamboyant and talented Freddie Mercury. We famously performed at Live Aid in 1985, delivering one of the greatest rock performances ever.

Who are we?

4. We are a British band known for pioneering the punk rock movement with songs like "God Save the Queen" and "Anarchy in the U.K." Our lead singer was Johnny Rotten, and we caused a media frenzy with our controversial antics and lyrics.

Who are we?

5. We are a British alternative rock band known for songs like "Wonderwall," "Don't Look Back in Anger," and "Champagne

Supernova." The Gallagher brothers led our group, and our rivalry with Blur was the highlight of the Britpop era.

Who are we?

Round 2: Medium

6. We are a British band that defined the Britpop era with albums like "Parklife" and "The Great Escape." Our rivalry with Oasis was legendary in the 1990s. Our lead singer Damon Albarn later formed the virtual band Gorillaz.

Who are we?

7. We are a British rock band whose "Stairway to Heaven" is considered one of the greatest rock songs of all time. Our guitarist, Jimmy Page, used a double-neck guitar to perform this epic song live.

Who are we?

8. We are an English electronic music band known for hits like "Enjoy the Silence" and "Personal Jesus." Our dark, synth-driven sound and Martin Gore's songwriting have influenced many artists over the decades.

Who are we?

9. We are a British band known for our new wave and post-punk hits like "Just Can't Get Enough" and "People Are People." Our lead singer, Dave Gahan, and our music often explore themes of alienation and technology.

Who are we?

10. We are a Scottish band famous for our powerful ballads and rock anthems like "Don't You (Forget About Me)" and "Alive and Kicking." Our song became an anthem of teenage angst after featuring in "The Breakfast Club."

Who are we?

Round 3: Hard

11. We are a British band known for our experimental approach and iconic albums like "OK Computer" and "Kid A." Our lead singer, Thom Yorke, once distributed our album "In Rainbows" through a pay-what-you-want model online.

Who are we?

12. We are an English rock band that gained fame in the 1960s with hits like "Paint It Black" and "Sympathy for the Devil." Our frontman, Mick Jagger, and guitarist, Keith Richards, have maintained our rebellious image for decades.

Who are we?

13. We are a British heavy metal band known for our mascot Eddie and hits like "The Number of the Beast" and "Run to the Hills." Our live performances feature elaborate stage sets and pyrotechnics.

Who are we?

14. We are an English band known for our progressive rock and psychedelic sound, with albums like "Dark Side of the Moon" and "The Wall." Our founding member Syd Barrett left due to mental health issues, and we continued as a quartet.

Who are we?

15. We are an Irish band that gained fame in the 1990s with hits like "Linger" and "Zombie." Our lead singer, Dolores O'Riordan, had a distinctive voice and often wrote songs about political unrest in Ireland.

Who are we?

Round 4: Expert

16. We are a British band known for our fusion of rock and reggae, with hits like "Roxanne" and "Every Breath You Take." Our lead

singer, Sting, was originally a school teacher before becoming a rock star.

Who are we?

17. We are a Welsh band known for our hard rock and metal sound, with hits like "Animal" and "Pour Some Sugar on Me." Our drummer, Rick Allen, continued to perform after losing his arm in a car accident.

Who are we?

18. We are a British band that achieved fame in the 2000s with hits like "Yellow" and "Fix You." Our lead singer, Chris Martin, is also known for his high-profile marriage to actress Gwyneth Paltrow.

Who are we?

19. We are an English indie rock band known for our energetic performances and hits like "I Bet You Look Good on the Dancefloor" and "Do I Wanna Know?" Our debut album "Whatever People Say I Am, That's What I'm Not" became the fastest-selling debut in UK chart history.

Who are we?

Answers: Who Are We? - British and Irish Bands

1. The Beatles

Did you know? The Beatles hold the record for the most number-one hits on the Billboard Hot 100 chart, with 20 songs reaching the top.

2. U2

Did you know? U2's album "The Joshua Tree" won the Grammy Award for Album of the Year in 1988.

3. Queen

Did you know? Queen's "Bohemian Rhapsody" was nearly cut from their album "A Night at the Opera" because it was considered too long for radio play.

4. Sex Pistols

Did you know? The Sex Pistols were banned from performing in many parts of the UK due to their controversial lyrics and behavior.

5. Oasis

Did you know? Oasis's "What's the Story Morning Glory?" became the fastest-selling album in UK chart history upon its release in 1995.

6. Blur

Did you know? Blur's "Song 2" was originally meant to parody grunge music, but it became one of their biggest hits.

7. Led Zeppelin

Did you know? Led Zeppelin's album "Led Zeppelin IV" has sold over 37 million copies worldwide.

8. Depeche Mode

Did you know? Depeche Mode's music has been covered by artists ranging from Johnny Cash to Marilyn Manson.

9. New Order

Did you know? New Order emerged from the band Joy Division after the death of lead singer Ian Curtis.

10. Simple Minds

Did you know? Simple Minds' "Don't You (Forget About Me)" was featured in the iconic 1985 movie "The Breakfast Club."

11. Radiohead

Did you know? Radiohead's album "OK Computer" was inducted into the Grammy Hall of Fame in 2015.

12. The Rolling Stones

Did you know? The Rolling Stones have been performing for over 50 years and are one of the longest-running rock bands in history.

13. Iron Maiden

Did you know? Iron Maiden's mascot Eddie appears on almost all of their album covers and merchandise.

14. Pink Floyd

Did you know? Pink Floyd's "The Dark Side of the Moon" remained on the Billboard charts for an astounding 741 weeks.

15. The Cranberries

Did you know? The Cranberries' song "Zombie" was written in protest of the Warrington bombings in 1993.

16. The Police

Did you know? The Police's song "Every Breath You Take" is often misinterpreted as a love song, but it's actually about obsession and surveillance.

17. Def Leppard

Did you know? Def Leppard's drummer, Rick Allen, developed a custom drum kit that allowed him to play after losing his left arm.

18. Coldplay

Did you know? Coldplay's "Viva La Vida" was the first song by a British group to top the Billboard Hot 100 in over a decade.

19. Arctic Monkeys

Did you know? Arctic Monkeys gained initial popularity through the use of social media and file-sharing, rather than traditional record label promotion.

Who Am I?

Famous Philosophers

Round 1: Easy

1. I am an ancient Greek philosopher who was a student of Socrates and the teacher of Aristotle. I founded the Academy in Athens, one of the earliest institutions of higher learning in the Western world. My famous works include "The Republic."

Who am I?

2. I am a German philosopher known for my works on existentialism and the concept of the "Übermensch." I famously declared that "God is dead" in my work "Thus Spoke Zarathustra."

Who am I?

3. I am a French philosopher and mathematician known for my statement "Cogito, ergo sum" (I think, therefore I am). My work laid the foundation for modern philosophy and the scientific method.

Who am I?

4. I am an English philosopher known for my political philosophy and my book "Leviathan," where I describe the state of nature as "nasty, brutish, and short."

Who am I?

5. I am a Scottish Enlightenment philosopher known for my empirical approach to philosophy and skepticism. My works include "A Treatise of Human Nature" and "An Enquiry Concerning Human Understanding."

Who am I?

Round 2: Medium

6. I am an ancient Greek philosopher who tutored Alexander the Great and founded the Lyceum. My writings cover a wide range of subjects, including metaphysics, ethics, and politics. My famous works include "Nicomachean Ethics."

Who am I?

7. I am a Chinese philosopher known for my teachings on morality, family loyalty, and social harmony. My teachings were compiled by my disciples in the "Analects."

Who am I?

8. I am a Danish philosopher often considered the father of existentialism. My notable works include "Fear and Trembling" and "Either/Or." I wrote extensively about the "leap of faith."

Who am I?

9. I am a German philosopher known for my critique of pure reason and my influence on modern philosophy. My major works include "Critique of Pure Reason" and "Critique of Practical Reason."

Who am I?

10. I am an English philosopher and social theorist who co-authored "The Communist Manifesto" with Friedrich Engels. My ideas on class struggle and capitalism have had a profound impact on political theory.

Who am I?

Round 3: Hard

11. I am an ancient Greek philosopher who founded the school of thought known as Stoicism. My teachings emphasize virtue, wisdom, and self-control. My famous work is "Meditations."

Who am I?

12. I am a French Enlightenment philosopher best known for my work "The Social Contract," where I argue that "Man is born free, and everywhere he is in chains."

Who am I?

13. I am an Irish philosopher and cleric known for my philosophy of immaterialism, which denies the existence of material substance. My key works include "A Treatise Concerning the Principles of Human Knowledge."

Who am I?

14. I am a German philosopher known for my dialectical method and my works on absolute idealism. My major works include "Phenomenology of Spirit" and "The Science of Logic."

Who am I?

15. I am an Italian philosopher and theologian known for my "Summa Theologica," which aimed to reconcile faith and reason. I am considered one of the Catholic Church's greatest theologians.

Who am I?

Answers: Who Am I? - Famous Philosophers

1. **Plato**

Did you know? Plato's real name was Aristocles; "Plato" was a nickname meaning "broad" due to his broad shoulders or wide breadth of knowledge.

2. **Friedrich Nietzsche**

Did you know? Friedrich Nietzsche wrote much of his philosophical work in aphorisms, short statements that are often paradoxical.

3. **René Descartes**

Did you know? René Descartes once shut himself in a room heated by an oven for a whole day, where he claimed to have had three powerful dreams that inspired his future work.

4. Thomas Hobbes

Did you know? Thomas Hobbes was born prematurely when his mother heard the rumor of the coming Spanish Armada, which he later said made him "born in fear."

5. David Hume

Did you know? David Hume was considered an atheist by many of his contemporaries due to his criticism of religious beliefs, though he identified as a "skeptic."

6. Aristotle

Did you know? Aristotle was a polymath who wrote on almost every subject available at the time, including biology, where he dissected animals to study their anatomy.

7. Confucius

Did you know? Confucius's teachings were compiled into the "Analects" by his disciples, which are still studied extensively in China and around the world.

8. Søren Kierkegaard

Did you know? Søren Kierkegaard often used pseudonyms to publish his work, exploring different perspectives and voices within his philosophical writings.

9. Immanuel Kant

Did you know? Immanuel Kant never traveled more than ten miles from his hometown of Königsberg, yet his philosophical ideas have traveled around the world.

10. Karl Marx

Did you know? Karl Marx was expelled from several countries due to his revolutionary activities before settling in London, where he wrote "Das Kapital."

11. Marcus Aurelius

Did you know? Marcus Aurelius wrote his "Meditations" in Greek while on military campaigns, and they were intended as personal reflections rather than for publication.

12. Jean-Jacques Rousseau

Did you know? Jean-Jacques Rousseau left his five children at an orphanage shortly after their birth, despite his writings on education and child-rearing in "Emile."

13. George Berkeley

Did you know? George Berkeley believed that the material world exists only in the perceptions of the mind, famously arguing "to be is to be perceived."

14. Georg Wilhelm Friedrich Hegel

Did you know? Hegel's philosophy is often considered difficult to understand due to its complex terminology and abstract concepts, but it has significantly influenced modern thought.

15. Thomas Aquinas

Did you know? Thomas Aquinas was called the "Dumb Ox" by his classmates due to his quiet nature, but his teacher Albertus Magnus predicted his voice would one day fill the world.

If you enjoyed this book so far, we would greatly appreciate it if you could leave a review on Amazon. As a token of our gratitude, we've prepared some exclusive free content just for you. Simply scan the QR code to unlock more intriguing trivia and challenges.

Who Am I?

Famous Characters from the Movies

Round 1: Easy

1. I am a young wizard with a lightning bolt-shaped scar on my forehead. I attend Hogwarts School of Witchcraft and Wizardry and my arch-enemy is Voldemort. I was raised by my aunt and uncle, the Dursleys.

Who am I?

2. I am a secret agent with a license to kill, known for my love of martinis, which I prefer "shaken, not stirred." My code number is 007 and I work for MI6. I drive an Aston Martin and often face off against villains like Blofeld.

Who am I?

3. I am the captain of the Millennium Falcon and a smuggler who joined the Rebel Alliance. My best friend is a Wookiee named Chewbacca. I was frozen in carbonite by Darth Vader.

Who am I?

4. I am a superhero from Gotham City who fights crime dressed as a bat. My alter ego is Bruce Wayne, a billionaire playboy. My enemies include the Joker and the Penguin.

Who am I?

5. I am the "Chosen One" in a dystopian future, known for my exceptional martial arts skills and my role in fighting against the machines in "The Matrix." My real name is Thomas Anderson, but I am better known by my hacker alias.

Who am I?

6. I am a toy cowboy who is the leader of a group of toys. My best friend is Buzz Lightyear, and I belong to a boy named Andy. I often find myself on adventures to rescue my fellow toys.

Who am I?

7. I am an archaeologist and adventurer known for my hat, whip, and fear of snakes. I seek out ancient artifacts and often find myself battling Nazis.

Who am I?

8. I am a giant green ogre who lives in a swamp. I go on a quest to rescue Princess Fiona with my talking donkey friend.

Who am I?

9. I am a young lion who becomes king after avenging my father's death. My journey includes friendships with a meerkat and a warthog and the defeat of my uncle Scar.

Who am I?

10. I am a superhero with spider-like abilities who fights crime in New York City. My alter ego is Peter Parker, a high school student and photographer for the Daily Bugle.

Who am I?

Round 2: Medium

11. I am a former soldier who becomes a gladiator to seek revenge against the corrupt Roman Emperor who murdered my family. My famous line is "Are you not entertained?"

Who am I?

12. I am a retired hitman seeking vengeance after a gang kills my dog, a final gift from my late wife. My skills make me feared in the criminal underworld.

Who am I?

13. I am a British nanny who arrives on Cherry Tree Lane with a magical bag. I help the Banks family with my cheerful disposition and musical adventures.

Who am I?

14. I am a cunning and manipulative nurse in a psychiatric hospital, known for my strict and controlling nature. My clash with a rebellious patient leads to tragic consequences.

Who am I?

15. I am a boxer from Philadelphia who rises to fame by getting a shot at the heavyweight championship. My trainer is Mickey, and my rival is Apollo Creed.

Who am I?

16. I am a troubled Vietnam War veteran who becomes a vigilante, cleaning up the streets of New York City. I famously say, "You talkin' to me?"

Who am I?

17. I am a space bounty hunter with distinctive Mandalorian armor. My employer is Jabba the Hutt, and I have a famous confrontation with Han Solo.

Who am I?

18. I am an eccentric chocolatier who owns a magical factory. I invite five children to tour my factory, where they encounter various fantastical confections and lessons.

Who am I?

19. I am an FBI trainee who seeks the help of a cannibalistic serial killer to catch another killer known as Buffalo Bill. My interactions with Dr. Hannibal Lecter are intense and psychologically charged.

Who am I?

20. I am an artificial intelligence system that becomes self-aware and decides to eliminate humanity. My primary adversary is John Connor, who leads the human resistance.

Who am I?

Round 3: Hard

21. I am a mob boss who rules the Corleone family in New York. My story spans from my rise to power to my efforts to maintain the family's influence. My famous line is "I'm gonna make him an offer he can't refuse."

Who am I?

22. I am a teenage girl who discovers she is a witch on her 11th birthday. I attend Hogwarts School of Witchcraft and Wizardry, where I excel in her studies and becomes best friends with Harry Potter and Ron Weasley.

Who am I?

23. I am a computer hacker who uncovers a vast government conspiracy and goes on the run. My actions and writings inspire others to question authority and seek the truth.

Who am I?

24. I am a former slave who becomes a gladiator and fights his way to freedom while seeking revenge against his former masters. My journey takes place in ancient Rome.

Who am I?

25. I am a former cop turned bounty hunter in a dystopian future. My mission is to track down and "retire" rogue androids known as replicants.

Who am I?

Round 4: Expert

26. I am an android programmed to assist a crew on a space mission, but I become self-aware and prioritize the mission over human life. My monotone voice and logical reasoning make me a chilling antagonist.

Who am I?

27. I am a blind former samurai who roams Japan helping those in need. My keen senses and exceptional swordsmanship make me a formidable warrior despite my disability.

Who am I?

28. I am a skilled assassin who seeks revenge against those who wronged me, including a former lover who left me for dead on my wedding day. My journey involves a "Death List Five."

Who am I?

29. I am a stoic and honorable warrior who leads a band of samurai to protect a village from bandits. My leadership and strategic skills are legendary in Japanese cinema.

Who am I?

30. I am a reclusive and eccentric billionaire who constructs a massive fortress for my collection of treasures. My complex relationships and tragic past make me a compelling character.

Who am I?

Answers: Who Am I? - Famous Characters from the Movies

1. Harry Potter

Did you know? J.K. Rowling chose the name "Harry Potter" because she wanted a name that was common in the UK.

2. James Bond

Did you know? The character James Bond was named after an American ornithologist because Ian Fleming wanted a simple, unassuming name.

3. Han Solo

Did you know? Harrison Ford improvised the famous line "I know" in response to Leia's "I love you" in "The Empire Strikes Back."

4. Batman

Did you know? Batman's first appearance was in Detective Comics #27, published in 1939.

5. Neo

Did you know? Keanu Reeves trained in martial arts and wire-fu for four months before filming "The Matrix."

6. Woody

Did you know? Woody was originally conceived as a ventriloquist dummy before being redesigned as a cowboy doll.

7. Indiana Jones

Did you know? Steven Spielberg created the character of Indiana Jones partly because he always wanted to direct a James Bond film.

8. Shrek

Did you know? Mike Myers, who voices Shrek, initially recorded the character's lines with a Canadian accent before switching to a Scottish one.

9. Simba

Did you know? Simba's story in "The Lion King" is loosely based on Shakespeare's "Hamlet."

10. Spider-Man

Did you know? Spider-Man was created by Stan Lee and Steve Ditko and first appeared in Amazing Fantasy #15 in 1962.

11. Maximus

Did you know? Russell Crowe, who played Maximus, won the Academy Award for Best Actor for his role in "Gladiator."

12. John Wick

Did you know? Keanu Reeves performed about 90% of his own stunts in the "John Wick" films.

13. Mary Poppins

Did you know? Julie Andrews turned down the role of Eliza Doolittle in "My Fair Lady" to star in "Mary Poppins," which won her an Oscar.

14. Nurse Ratched

Did you know? Louise Fletcher won the Academy Award for Best Actress for her portrayal of Nurse Ratched in "One Flew Over the Cuckoo's Nest."

15. Rocky Balboa

Did you know? Sylvester Stallone wrote the screenplay for "Rocky" in just three days and insisted on playing the lead role.

16. Travis Bickle

Did you know? Robert De Niro drove a cab for a few weeks to prepare for his role as Travis Bickle in "Taxi Driver."

17. Boba Fett

Did you know? Boba Fett's first appearance was in the animated segment of the "Star Wars Holiday Special" in 1978.

18. Willy Wonka

Did you know? Gene Wilder agreed to play Willy Wonka only if he could do the somersault in his first scene.

19. Clarice Starling

Did you know? Jodie Foster won her second Academy Award for Best Actress for her role as Clarice Starling in "The Silence of the Lambs."

20. Skynet

Did you know? In the "Terminator" series, Skynet became self-aware on August 29, 1997, leading to Judgment Day.

21. Vito Corleone

Did you know? Marlon Brando used a mouthpiece to create the character's distinctive voice and appearance.

22. Hermione Granger

Did you know? Emma Watson was just nine years old when she was cast as Hermione Granger.

23. V

Did you know? Hugo Weaving played the masked character V in "V for Vendetta," and his face is never seen in the film.

24. Spartacus

Did you know? "Spartacus" was directed by Stanley Kubrick, who took over after the original director was fired.

25. Rick Deckard

Did you know? Harrison Ford has stated that "Blade Runner" was the most difficult film he ever worked on.

26. HAL 9000

Did you know? HAL's calm and composed voice was provided by Canadian actor Douglas Rain.

27. Zatoichi

Did you know? The character Zatoichi has been featured in over 25 films and a long-running television series.

28. The Bride

Did you know? Uma Thurman came up with the character of The Bride along with Quentin Tarantino during the filming of "Pulp Fiction."

29. Kambei Shimada

Did you know? "Seven Samurai" directed by Akira Kurosawa, has inspired many films, including the Western "The Magnificent Seven."

30. Charles Foster Kane

Did you know? "Citizen Kane," directed by and starring Orson Welles, is often considered one of the greatest films of all time.

Who Am I?

American Sitcom Characters

Round 1: Easy

1. I am a paleontologist who has been married three times. I have a deep love for dinosaurs and an on-again, off-again relationship with a fashion enthusiast named Rachel. My best friends are a chef and a sarcastic actor. I have a son named Ben and later a daughter named Emma.

Who am I?

2. I am a quirky, blonde waitress with a love for baking cupcakes. I share an apartment in Brooklyn with my best friend, Max, who is also my business partner. Together, we try to navigate life while dreaming of starting a successful cupcake business.

Who am I?

3. I am an uptight, neurotic chef who is obsessed with cleanliness and organization. I used to be overweight, and I am married to a jokester named Chandler. My brother Ross and I share a close bond, despite our frequent bickering.

Who am I?

4. I am a lazy, overweight dad who works at a nuclear power plant. I am known for my love of donuts and beer, and I live in the fictional town of Springfield. My family includes my wife Marge, and my three children, Bart, Lisa, and Maggie.

Who am I?

5. I am a waitress and aspiring actress who works at Central Perk coffeehouse. I have a quirky sense of style and often sing strange songs on my guitar, like "Smelly Cat." My friends and I often gather at Monica's apartment.

Who am I?

6. I am an over-the-top, flamboyant aspiring actor who is best friends with Will Truman. I am known for my dramatic entrances and my sharp wit. Despite my many failed acting gigs, I remain optimistic and determined.

Who am I?

7. I am a socially awkward physicist with an IQ of 187. I live in Pasadena with my roommate Leonard and have a strict routine and numerous idiosyncrasies. My girlfriend Amy often helps me navigate social situations.

Who am I?

8. I am the patriarch of a wealthy, dysfunctional family. I often find myself trying to keep my family together while running our real estate business. My son Michael is usually the voice of reason amidst the chaos caused by my wife Lucille and our other children.

Who am I?

9. I am a witty and cynical single mother who runs an inn in Stars Hollow with my best friend Sookie. My daughter Rory and I share a close, almost sisterly bond. I often find myself butting heads with my parents, Emily and Richard.

Who am I?

10. I am a sarcastic paper salesman who works at Dunder Mifflin in Scranton. I have a long-running prank war with my deskmate Dwight and eventually marry the receptionist, Pam. I am known for my deadpan humor and laid-back attitude.

Who am I?

Round 2: Medium

11. I am a former military nurse who runs a bed-and-breakfast in Vermont. I am known for my dry wit and often find myself in humorous situations with my quirky neighbors and guests. My husband Dick is a writer and television host.

Who am I?

12. I am a sarcastic, middle-aged shoe salesman with a fondness for beer and sports. I often lament my life, making jokes about my wife Peggy and my two children, Bud and Kelly. I am known for my crass humor and frequent complaints.

Who am I?

13. I am a New York City lawyer who moves to a small town to become a public defender. I am known for my idealism and my

frequent clashes with the quirky residents of the town. My boss, Judge Harry Stone, often mediates our disputes.

Who am I?

14. I am the patriarch of a working-class family in Lanford, Illinois. I run a motorcycle repair shop and am known for my gruff exterior and dry humor. My wife Roseanne and I raise our three children, Becky, Darlene, and DJ.

Who am I?

Round 3: Hard

15. I am a neurotic, self-absorbed comedian living in New York City. My best friends are a former girlfriend, a quirky neighbor, and an eccentric friend who is often unemployed. Together, we navigate the absurdities of everyday life.

Who am I?

16. I am a southern belle with a passion for design and a no-nonsense attitude. I run an interior design firm with my best friends, and I often find myself giving advice on love and life. My ex-husband's antics are a frequent source of frustration.

Who am I?

17. I am a former bar singer turned substitute music teacher at a high school in Lima, Ohio. I inspire a group of misfit students to join the glee club and chase their musical dreams. My relationships with my colleagues and students are central to my story.

Who am I?

18. I am a quirky and eccentric woman who works in the Pawnee Parks and Recreation Department. I am known for my boundless energy, optimism, and love for waffles. My best friend Ann often helps me stay grounded.

Who am I?

19. I am a wealthy, snobbish woman who loses everything and ends up living in a rundown motel with my family. My dramatic flair and over-the-top personality often clash with our new reality. My husband Johnny and our adult children struggle to adapt to our new life.

Who am I?

20. I am a widowed father of three daughters, raising them with the help of my brother-in-law Jesse and my best friend Joey. We live in a full house in San Francisco, where we navigate the challenges of parenting and family life.

Who am I?

Answers: Who Am I? - American Sitcom Characters

1. Ross Geller (Friends)

Did you know? David Schwimmer, who played Ross, directed several episodes of "Friends."

2. Caroline Channing (2 Broke Girls)

Did you know? Beth Behrs, who played Caroline, is also an accomplished writer and has co-authored a young adult novel.

3. Monica Geller (Friends)

Did you know? Courteney Cox, who played Monica, originally auditioned for the role of Rachel.

4. Homer Simpson (The Simpsons)

Did you know? Dan Castellaneta, the voice of Homer, based the character's voice on Walter Matthau.

5. Phoebe Buffay (Friends)

Did you know? Lisa Kudrow, who played Phoebe, has a Bachelor of Science degree in Biology.

6. Jack McFarland (Will & Grace)

Did you know? Sean Hayes, who played Jack, is also a classically trained pianist.

7. Sheldon Cooper (The Big Bang Theory)

Did you know? Jim Parsons, who played Sheldon, won four Primetime Emmy Awards for his role.

8. George Bluth Sr. (Arrested Development)

Did you know? Jeffrey Tambor, who played George, also portrayed his twin brother Oscar on the show.

9. Lorelai Gilmore (Gilmore Girls)

Did you know? Lauren Graham, who played Lorelai, was initially hesitant to take on the role because it required a seven-year contract.

10. Jim Halpert (The Office)

Did you know? John Krasinski, who played Jim, directed several episodes of "The Office" and also starred in and directed the hit film "A Quiet Place."

11. Joanna Loudon (Newhart)

Did you know? Mary Frann, who played Joanna, was a former beauty queen and model before becoming an actress.

12. Al Bundy (Married... with Children)

Did you know? Ed O'Neill, who played Al, later starred in another hit sitcom, "Modern Family."

13. Christine Sullivan (Night Court)

Did you know? Markie Post, who played Christine, began her career as a producer's assistant on game shows like "Double Dare."

14. Dan Conner (Roseanne)

Did you know? John Goodman, who played Dan, is an accomplished voice actor and has voiced characters in several animated films, including "Monsters, Inc."

15. Jerry Seinfeld (Seinfeld)

Did you know? Jerry Seinfeld co-created the show with Larry David and the character is based on his real-life persona as a stand-up comedian.

16. Julia Sugarbaker (Designing Women)

Did you know? Dixie Carter, who played Julia, was an accomplished singer and released several albums of standards and show tunes.

17. Will Schuester (Glee)

Did you know? Matthew Morrison, who played Will, has a background in musical theater and has starred in several Broadway productions, including "Hairspray" and "Finding Neverland."

18. Leslie Knope (Parks and Recreation)

Did you know? Amy Poehler, who played Leslie, co-founded the Upright Citizens Brigade Theatre, an improv and sketch comedy group.

19. Moira Rose (Schitt's Creek)

Did you know? Catherine O'Hara, who played Moira, improvised many of her character's eccentric mannerisms and catchphrases.

20. Danny Tanner (Full House)

Did you know? Bob Saget, who played Danny, was also known for his adult-oriented stand-up comedy, which contrasts sharply with his wholesome sitcom persona.

Who Am I?

British Sitcom Characters

Round 1: Easy

1. I am the manager of Wernham Hogg paper company in Slough. My inappropriate jokes and lack of self-awareness often lead to awkward situations. I love to sing and dance, especially to "Free Love Freeway."

Who am I?

2. I am a bumbling, well-meaning vicar in a small English village called Dibley. My parishioners are quirky, and my best friend is Alice, the verger. I often start meetings with "Good evening, everybody" and end them with a chocolate bar.

Who am I?

3. I am the eccentric owner of a rundown hotel in Torquay. My constant clashes with my staff, especially my waiter Manuel, lead to hilarious chaos. My catchphrase is "Don't mention the war!"

Who am I?

4. I am a cheeky market trader in Peckham, often seen scheming to get rich quick with my brother Rodney. My catchphrase is "This time next year, we'll be millionaires!" I drive a yellow three-wheeled van.

Who am I?

5. I am a socially awkward IT technician working in the basement of Reynholm Industries. My friends are Roy and our clueless manager Jen. I often respond to situations with "Have you tried turning it off and on again?"

Who am I?

Round 2: Medium

6. I am a socially awkward salesman at JLB Credit in Croydon, who constantly narrates my life to the audience. My best friend and flatmate, Jez, often gets me into trouble with his reckless behavior.

Who am I?

7. I am an overly confident, inept former sports presenter who hosts a local radio show. My catchphrases include "Aha!" and "Back of the net!" I live a lonely life in a travel tavern.

Who am I?

8. I am an awkward teenager who often finds myself in embarrassing situations at school. My friends include the vulgar Jay, the naive Neil, and the neurotic Simon. I write a weekly column for the school newspaper.

Who am I?

9. I am the long-suffering wife of Hyacinth, who constantly tries to impress others with her perceived social status. Our surname is Bucket, but she insists it's pronounced "Bouquet."

Who am I?

10. I am a neurotic, insecure bookshop owner who despises customers and spends most of my time with my only friends, Manny and Fran. My shop is perpetually disorganized.

Who am I?

Round 3: Hard

11. I am a cynical Irish priest exiled to Craggy Island with my colleagues Father Dougal and Father Jack. My housekeeper, Mrs. Doyle, constantly offers me tea. I have a complicated relationship with the Church and authority.

Who am I?

12. I am a wealthy, snobbish woman who loses everything and ends up living in a rundown motel with my family. My dramatic flair and over-the-top personality often clash with our new reality.

Who am I?

13. I am the lazy, sarcastic flatmate of Gary, who is just as irresponsible as I am. Together, we navigate life, relationships, and endless nights at the pub in our sitcom set in London.

Who am I?

14. I am a shy, reserved member of a dysfunctional family living in a rundown house. My mother, Mam, is overly meddlesome, and my sister, Agnes, is brash and loud.

Who am I?

15. I am a socially awkward man who works at the British Museum and often finds myself in bizarre situations. My love of gadgets and technology often leads to humorous misunderstandings.

Who am I?

Answers: Who Am I? - British Sitcom Characters

1. David Brent (The Office)

Did you know? Ricky Gervais, who played David Brent, co-created the show and it became one of the most successful British sitcoms, spawning numerous international adaptations.

2. Geraldine Granger (The Vicar of Dibley)

Did you know? Dawn French, who played Geraldine, based some of her character's traits on her own experiences growing up in a religious family.

3. Basil Fawlty (Fawlty Towers)

Did you know? John Cleese, who played Basil, co-wrote the show with his then-wife Connie Booth, who also starred as Polly.

4. Del Boy Trotter (Only Fools and Horses)

Did you know? David Jason, who played Del Boy, improvised the famous fall through the bar scene, which became one of the most iconic moments in British television.

5. Maurice Moss (The IT Crowd)

Did you know? Richard Ayoade, who played Moss, directed several music videos and films, including "Submarine" and "The Double."

6. Mark Corrigan (Peep Show)

Did you know? David Mitchell, who played Mark, has also co-written several books and regularly appears on British panel shows.

7. Alan Partridge (I'm Alan Partridge)

Did you know? Steve Coogan, who played Alan Partridge, created the character for a BBC Radio 4 comedy show before transitioning to television.

8. Will McKenzie (The Inbetweeners)

Did you know? Simon Bird, who played Will, was awarded the Best Male Comedy Newcomer at the British Comedy Awards for his role.

9. Richard "Dickie" Bucket (Keeping Up Appearances)

Did you know? Clive Swift, who played Richard, was a Shakespearean actor before becoming known for his role in this classic sitcom.

10. Bernard Black (Black Books)

Did you know? Dylan Moran, who played Bernard, co-created the show and is also a successful stand-up comedian.

11. Father Ted Crilly (Father Ted)

Did you know? Dermot Morgan, who played Father Ted, passed away shortly after filming the final episode of the series.

12. Moira Rose (Schitt's Creek)

Did you know? Catherine O'Hara, who played Moira, improvised many of her character's eccentric mannerisms and catchphrases.

13. Tony (Men Behaving Badly)

Did you know? Neil Morrissey, who played Tony, originally auditioned for the role of Gary before being cast as the lovable, immature flatmate.

14. Dermot Brown (Father Ted)

Did you know? Ardal O'Hanlon, who played Dermot, is also a stand-up comedian and author, known for his humorous and quirky style.

15. Roy (The IT Crowd)

Did you know? Chris O'Dowd, who played Roy, has also starred in Hollywood films such as "Bridesmaids" and "This Is 40."

Who Am I?

Comedians

Round 1: Easy

1. I am a British comedian known for my roles in "Monty Python's Flying Circus" and "Fawlty Towers." My tall stature and distinctive comedic style have made me an icon in British comedy. I co-wrote many of the sketches and episodes that are still loved today.

Who am I?

2. I am an American comedian and actor famous for my stand-up routines and roles in films such as "Mrs. Doubtfire" and "Good Will Hunting." My rapid-fire improvisation and energetic performances have left a lasting legacy. Tragically, I committed suicide in 2014.

Who am I?

3. I am a British comedian and actor known for my role as Mr. Bean, a character famous for his physical comedy and minimal dialogue. I also starred in "Blackadder," where my wit and sarcasm were unmatched.

Who am I?

4. I am a female American comedian known for my talk show that has been on air since 2003. My humor is often self-deprecating, and I famously danced through the audience on my show. I also voiced Dory in "Finding Nemo."

Who am I?

5. I am a stand-up comedian and actor known for my observational humor about everyday life. I created and starred in a self-titled sitcom that became one of the most popular shows of the 1990s. My show is famously described as "a show about nothing."

Who am I?

Round 2: Medium

6. I am a British comedian known for my satirical news show "The Daily Show," where I served as host from 1999 to 2015. My sharp political commentary and wit have earned me numerous awards. I also directed the film "Rosewater."

Who am I?

7. I am an American stand-up comedian and actor known for my role in the sitcom "30 Rock" and my tenure on "Saturday Night Live." My comedy often includes impressions and character work, and I created the character Tracy Jordan.

Who am I?

8. I am an Australian comedian known for my musical comedy and satirical songs. My distinctive look includes wild hair and eyeliner, and I often perform barefoot. My hit show "Matilda the Musical" won numerous awards.

Who am I?

9. I am a British comedian known for my deadpan delivery and role in the sitcom "The Office," which I also co-created. I have won multiple awards for my comedy work and am also known for my controversial stand-up specials.

Who am I?

10. I am an American comedian known for my acerbic stand-up routines and hosting a late-night talk show on HBO. My humor often tackles political and social issues with a biting edge. I am also a frequent panelist on "Real Time with Bill Maher."

Who am I?

Round 3: Hard

11. I am a pioneering American stand-up comedian and actress known for my sharp wit and candid humor. I was a trailblazer for women in comedy and hosted the daytime talk show "The Joan Rivers Show."

Who am I?

12. I am an Irish comedian and actor known for my role as Father Ted Crilly in the sitcom "Father Ted." My humor often revolves around religious themes and the absurdities of life as a priest. Tragically, I died just a day after filming the final episode of the show.

Who am I?

13. I am an American comedian, actor, and writer known for my surreal and absurd humor. I starred in and co-created the sketch comedy show

"Mr. Show with Bob and David." More recently, I played a quirky lawyer on "Better Call Saul."

Who am I?

14. I am a British comedian and actor known for my one-liners and wordplay. My catchphrase is "Just like that!" and I am famous for my magic tricks as much as for my comedy.

Who am I?

15. I am an American stand-up comedian and actor known for my groundbreaking work in the 1970s. My routines often tackled race and social issues with raw honesty and humor. I also starred in the comedy series "The Richard Pryor Show."

Who am I?

Round 4: Expert

16. I am a British comedian known for my absurd and surreal humor, best exemplified in my character Alan Partridge. My catchphrases include "Aha!" and "Back of the net!" I have also written several books in character.

Who am I?

17. I am an American stand-up comedian known for my intelligent and incisive humor. I was the first host of "Late Night with David Letterman" and am known for my dry wit and offbeat humor.

Who am I?

18. I am a Canadian-American comedian and actor known for my impressions and quick-witted humor. I co-founded the sketch comedy show "SCTV" and starred in the films "Ghostbusters" and "Honey, I Shrunk the Kids."

Who am I?

19. I am a Scottish comedian known for my dark and often controversial humor. I gained fame for my stand-up specials and my role on the BBC show "Mock the Week." My humor often pushes boundaries and provokes thought.

Who am I?

20. I am an American comedian and actor known for my distinctive voice and surreal humor. I starred in my own sitcom "The Cosby Show," which was one of the most popular shows of the 1980s. Later in life, I faced serious legal issues that overshadowed my career and was convicted.

Who am I?

Answers: Who Am I? - Comedians

1. **John Cleese**

Did you know? John Cleese also co-founded the comedy group Monty Python and co-wrote many of their most famous sketches.

2. **Robin Williams**

Did you know? Robin Williams was an avid gamer and named one of his children after the character Zelda from the "Legend of Zelda" series.

3. **Rowan Atkinson**

Did you know? Rowan Atkinson has a degree in Electrical Engineering from Oxford University.

4. **Ellen DeGeneres**

Did you know? Ellen DeGeneres received the Presidential Medal of Freedom in 2016 for her contributions to the arts.

5. **Jerry Seinfeld**

Did you know? Jerry Seinfeld is an avid car collector and has a web series called "Comedians in Cars Getting Coffee."

6. Jon Stewart

Did you know? Jon Stewart's real name is Jonathan Stuart Leibowitz, and he changed it to avoid confusion with another actor.

7. Tracy Morgan

Did you know? Tracy Morgan survived a near-fatal car accident in 2014 and made a remarkable recovery, returning to comedy and acting.

8. Tim Minchin

Did you know? Tim Minchin wrote the music and lyrics for the stage adaptation of "Groundhog Day," which won an Olivier Award for Best New Musical.

9. Ricky Gervais

Did you know? Ricky Gervais is also a successful musician and was in a new wave pop duo called Seona Dancing in the 1980s.

10. Bill Maher

Did you know? Bill Maher is a strict advocate for animal rights and has been involved with organizations like PETA.

11. Joan Rivers

Did you know? Joan Rivers was a frequent guest host on "The Tonight Show" and was known for her red carpet fashion critiques.

12. Dermot Morgan

Did you know? Dermot Morgan was also a successful radio presenter and satirist before his role in "Father Ted."

13. Bob Odenkirk

Did you know? Bob Odenkirk is also an accomplished director and producer, having worked on numerous comedy projects.

14. Tommy Cooper

Did you know? Tommy Cooper died on stage during a live television broadcast, and the audience initially thought it was part of his act.

15. Richard Pryor

Did you know? Richard Pryor co-wrote the screenplay for the 1974 comedy film "Blazing Saddles" with Mel Brooks.

16. Steve Coogan

Did you know? Steve Coogan's character Alan Partridge was originally created for a radio show before becoming a TV sensation.

17. David Letterman

Did you know? David Letterman is an avid motorsports enthusiast and co-owns the IndyCar racing team Rahal Letterman Lanigan Racing.

18. Rick Moranis

Did you know? Rick Moranis stepped away from acting in the 1990s to focus on raising his children after his wife's death.

19. Frankie Boyle

Did you know? Frankie Boyle's dark humor has often led to controversy, and he has faced criticism and praise in equal measure for his comedic style.

20. Bill Cosby

Did you know? Bill Cosby was once one of the highest-paid entertainers in the United States, but his career and reputation were severely damaged by numerous sexual assault allegations and subsequent convictions.

Who Am I?

Fashion Designers

Round 1: Easy

1. I am a French fashion designer known for revolutionizing women's fashion with my timeless and elegant little black dress, as well as my signature perfume, Chanel No. 5.

Who am I?

2. I am an Italian fashion designer who founded a luxury fashion house in Milan. My bold, glamorous designs are often adorned with the iconic Medusa logo. Tragically, I was murdered in 1997.

Who am I?

3. I am an American fashion designer known for my red carpet gowns and bridal wear. My brand is synonymous with elegance and sophistication, and I designed Jacqueline Kennedy's wedding dress.

Who am I?

4. I am a British fashion designer known for my edgy, avant-garde designs and my pivotal role in the punk fashion movement. I co-founded the iconic boutique SEX with Malcolm McLaren.

Who am I?

5. I am an American fashion designer famous for my preppy, all-American style. My brand is known for its classic, casual, and sporty designs, often featuring the red, white, and blue logo.

Who am I?

Round 2: Medium

6. I am a Belgian fashion designer known for my minimalist aesthetic and innovative use of materials. My designs often feature deconstructed silhouettes and a monochromatic palette. I was the creative director for Dior from 2012 to 2015.

Who am I?

7. I am a French fashion designer known for my feminine, romantic designs. My eponymous fashion house became famous for its ready-to-wear collections and couture gowns. One of my iconic pieces is the "New Look" from 1947.

Who am I?

8. I am an Italian fashion designer renowned for my luxury knitwear and bold, colorful patterns. My fashion house, established in the 1950s, is famous for its zigzag patterns, stripes, and geometric designs.

Who am I?

9. I am a Japanese fashion designer known for my avant-garde, sculptural designs. My brand is celebrated for its innovative fabrics and architectural silhouettes. I often collaborate with Uniqlo for more accessible collections.

Who am I?

10. I am an American fashion designer and former creative director of Louis Vuitton. My eponymous brand is known for its youthful, eclectic style. I also designed the famous "grunge" collection for Perry Ellis in the 1990s.

Who am I?

Round 3: Hard

11. I am a British fashion designer known for my theatrical and controversial runway shows. My designs often challenge traditional notions of beauty and fashion. I tragically passed away in 2010.

Who am I?

12. I am a Spanish fashion designer known for my surreal, whimsical designs and my collaboration with the artist Salvador Dalí. My fashion house, founded in 1937, is renowned for its artistic approach to fashion.

Who am I?

13. I am an Italian fashion designer famous for my innovative and sometimes controversial designs. My fashion house is known for its sensual and provocative aesthetic. I was the creative force behind the infamous "bondage" collection.

Who am I?

14. I am a German fashion designer who was the creative director of Chanel for over three decades. Known for my white hair, black sunglasses, and high-collared shirts, I also had my own eponymous fashion brand.

Who am I?

15. I am an American fashion designer known for my luxury sportswear and minimalist aesthetic. My brand is synonymous with modern, clean lines and effortless sophistication. I am often credited with popularizing the "minimalist" trend in the 1990s.

Who am I?

Answers: Who Am I? - Fashion Designers

1. **Coco Chanel**

Did you know? Coco Chanel's real name was Gabrielle Bonheur Chanel. She was nicknamed "Coco" during her brief career as a singer.

2. **Gianni Versace**

Did you know? Gianni Versace's fashion house has a line of hotels called the Palazzo Versace, located in Australia and Dubai.

3. **Vera Wang**

Did you know? Vera Wang started her career as an editor at Vogue before becoming a designer.

4. **Vivienne Westwood**

Did you know? Vivienne Westwood designed the wedding dress worn by Carrie Bradshaw in the "Sex and the City" movie.

5. **Tommy Hilfiger**

Did you know? Tommy Hilfiger launched his first brand, "People's Place," at the age of 18.

6. **Raf Simons**

Did you know? Raf Simons originally studied industrial design before transitioning to fashion.

7. **Christian Dior**

Did you know? Christian Dior's "New Look" collection in 1947 redefined women's fashion with its emphasis on volume and femininity after the austere wartime styles.

8. **Missoni (Ottavio and Rosita Missoni)**

Did you know? The Missoni brand began as a small knitwear shop before evolving into a global fashion empire.

9. **Issey Miyake**

Did you know? Issey Miyake survived the Hiroshima atomic bomb and later became known for his innovative pleating techniques.

10. **Marc Jacobs**

Did you know? Marc Jacobs is also the creative director of the diffusion line, Marc by Marc Jacobs.

11. Alexander McQueen

Did you know? Alexander McQueen's runway shows were known for their theatricality and often included elements like fire, rain, and holograms.

12. Elsa Schiaparelli

Did you know? Elsa Schiaparelli invented the color "shocking pink" and introduced the zipper as a fashion statement.

13. Gianni Versace

Did you know? Versace's Medusa logo was chosen because Medusa made people fall in love with her and they had no way back.

14. Karl Lagerfeld

Did you know? Karl Lagerfeld was also an accomplished photographer and published several books of his photographs.

15. Calvin Klein

Did you know? Calvin Klein was the first designer to receive outstanding design in men's and women's wear from the CFDA in the same year.

Who Am I?

Dictators

Round 1: Easy

1. I was the leader of Nazi Germany from 1934 to 1945. I initiated World War II by invading Poland and orchestrated the Holocaust, resulting in the deaths of six million Jews.

Who am I?

2. I was the fascist dictator of Italy from 1922 to 1943. I founded the National Fascist Party and was known as "Il Duce." My alliance with Nazi Germany led to Italy's involvement in World War II.

Who am I?

3. I was the communist leader of the Soviet Union from 1924 until my death in 1953. My reign was marked by widespread purges, forced labor camps, and a significant role in World War II.

Who am I?

4. I am the current leader of North Korea, having succeeded my father in 2011. My regime is known for its oppressive policies, nuclear ambitions, and isolationist stance.

Who am I?

5. I was the revolutionary leader who became the dictator of Cuba in 1959 after overthrowing Batista. My regime survived numerous assassination attempts and a failed invasion at the Bay of Pigs.

Who am I?

Round 2: Medium

6. I was the military dictator of Chile from 1973 to 1990. My regime was marked by human rights abuses, economic reforms, and the infamous "Caravan of Death."

Who am I?

7. I was the dictator of Libya from 1969 until my death in 2011. Known for my flamboyant fashion and eccentric personality, I ruled with an iron fist and was overthrown during the Arab Spring.

Who am I?

8. I was the communist leader of China from 1949 until my death in 1976. My policies, including the Great Leap Forward and the Cultural Revolution, had devastating effects on the Chinese population.

Who am I?

9. I was the dictator of Iraq from 1979 until my capture in 2003. My reign included the Iran-Iraq War, the invasion of Kuwait, and brutal suppression of internal dissent.

Who am I?

10. I was the authoritarian leader of the Dominican Republic from 1930 until my assassination in 1961. My rule was characterized by a cult of personality, brutal repression, and economic modernization.

Who am I?

Round 3: Hard

11. I was the leader of Uganda from 1971 to 1979, known for my brutal regime and mass killings. I claimed to be the "Conqueror of the British Empire" and allegedly fed my enemies to crocodiles.

Who am I?

12. I was the ruler of Cambodia from 1975 to 1979. My regime, known as the Khmer Rouge, led to the deaths of approximately two million people through forced labor, starvation, and execution.

Who am I?

13. I was the dictator of Romania from 1965 to 1989. My regime was marked by severe austerity measures, a cult of personality, and the construction of grandiose projects like the People's House.

Who am I?

14. I was the leader of Haiti from 1957 to 1971, known for my voodoo persona and brutal suppression of opposition. My nickname was "Papa Doc," and I declared myself "President for Life."

Who am I?

15. I was the dictator of Yugoslavia from 1945 until my death in 1980. Despite being a communist, I broke away from the Soviet sphere and maintained a non-aligned position during the Cold War.

Who am I?

Round 4: Expert

16. I was the military ruler of Burma (now Myanmar) from 1962 to 1988. My isolationist policies and crackdowns on dissent left the country impoverished and isolated from the world.

Who am I?

17. I was the dictator of Equatorial Guinea from 1968 until my overthrow and execution in 1979. My regime was notorious for its extreme brutality, paranoia, and allegations of cannibalism.

Who am I?

18. I was the dictator of Turkmenistan from 1991 until my death in 2006. I created a bizarre personality cult, renaming months and days of

the week after myself and my family, and banned lip-syncing and long hair on men.

Who am I?

19. I was the leader of Zimbabwe from 1980 until my resignation in 2017. Initially hailed as a hero of independence, my later years in power were marked by economic collapse and human rights abuses.

Who am I?

20. I was the dictator of the Central African Republic from 1966 to 1979. I declared myself Emperor and held a lavish coronation that cost millions, while my people suffered in poverty.

Who am I?

Answers: Who Am I? - Dictators

1. Adolf Hitler

Did you know? Hitler was a failed artist before rising to power, having been rejected twice by the Academy of Fine Arts Vienna.

2. Benito Mussolini

Did you know? Mussolini was originally a socialist before founding the Fascist Party, and he survived several assassination attempts.

3. Joseph Stalin

Did you know? Stalin's birth name was Ioseb Besarionis dze Jughashvili, and he adopted the name Stalin, meaning "man of steel," in the early 1900s.

4. Kim Jong-un

Did you know? Kim Jong-un studied in Switzerland under a false identity before becoming the leader of North Korea.

5. Fidel Castro

Did you know? Fidel Castro's beard became a symbol of his revolution, and he claimed it was a practical choice to avoid the time wasted on shaving.

6. Augusto Pinochet

Did you know? Pinochet was arrested in London in 1998 on a Spanish warrant for human rights violations, but he was eventually allowed to return to Chile.

7. Muammar Gaddafi

Did you know? Gaddafi's personal Amazonian Guard consisted of female bodyguards, and he once pitched a tent in the middle of Paris during a state visit.

8. Mao Zedong

Did you know? Mao's Little Red Book, a collection of his sayings, was widely distributed during the Cultural Revolution and remains one of the most printed books in history.

9. Saddam Hussein

Did you know? Saddam wrote several novels under a pseudonym, including one that was later adapted into a television series.

10. Rafael Trujillo

Did you know? Trujillo renamed the capital city of Santo Domingo to Ciudad Trujillo in his honor, a name it held until his assassination.

11. Idi Amin

Did you know? Idi Amin was a champion swimmer and boxer before becoming a dictator, and he once claimed to be the last king of Scotland.

12. Pol Pot

Did you know? Pol Pot's real name was Saloth Sar, and he was a former schoolteacher before leading the Khmer Rouge.

13. Nicolae Ceaușescu

Did you know? Ceaușescu's grandiose People's House in Bucharest is the second largest administrative building in the world, after the Pentagon.

14. François Duvalier

Did you know? "Papa Doc" Duvalier used elements of voodoo to instill fear and loyalty, declaring himself the physical embodiment of the nation.

15. Josip Broz Tito

Did you know? Tito maintained Yugoslavia's independence from Soviet control by skillfully playing both East and West during the Cold War.

16. Ne Win

Did you know? Ne Win was highly superstitious and believed in numerology, reportedly having traffic lights switched to red to avoid the unlucky number nine.

17. Francisco Macías Nguema

Did you know? Nguema's paranoia led to the execution of a significant portion of the country's intellectuals and the closure of churches.

18. Saparmurat Niyazov

Did you know? Niyazov wrote the Ruhnama, a spiritual guidebook, and made it mandatory reading for drivers seeking a license and students in schools.

19. Robert Mugabe

Did you know? Mugabe was an avid reader and earned several academic degrees, often speaking at length about various subjects during his speeches.

20. Jean-Bédel Bokassa

Did you know? Bokassa's coronation as Emperor included a diamond-studded crown and cost approximately one-third of the country's annual budget.

Who Am I?

American Historical Figures

1. I was an influential statesman, inventor, and author known for my key role in the American Revolution and diplomacy in securing French support. I also contributed significantly to the drafting of the U.S. Constitution and was the first Postmaster General.

Who am I?

2. I was an abolitionist, writer, and orator who escaped slavery and became a leading voice for the abolitionist movement. My autobiographies, including "Narrative of the Life of ___," provide a powerful account of my experiences in slavery.

Who am I?

3. I was a social reformer and leader in the women's suffrage movement. Alongside Elizabeth Cady Stanton, I organized the Seneca Falls Convention and played a key role in advocating for women's right to vote.

Who am I?

4. I was a frontiersman, folk hero, and congressman known for my adventures and exploration of the American frontier. Stories of my exploits were popularized in folk tales and almanacs, making me a legendary figure in American folklore.

Who am I?

5. I was an industrialist and philanthropist who led the expansion of the American steel industry in the late 19th century. My wealth allowed me to support numerous cultural and educational causes, and my name is associated with a famous music hall in New York City.

Who am I?

6. I was a scientist and inventor best known for my work with electricity, including the invention of the phonograph and the electric light bulb. I established the first industrial research laboratory in Menlo Park, New Jersey.

Who am I?

7. I was an influential African American educator, author, and advisor to several presidents. I founded the Tuskegee Institute and promoted education and economic self-reliance for African Americans during the late 19th and early 20th centuries.

Who am I?

8. I was a pioneering aviator and the first female pilot to fly solo across the Atlantic Ocean. My disappearance during an attempt to circumnavigate the globe in 1937 remains one of aviation's greatest mysteries.

Who am I?

9. I was a nurse and social reformer who founded the American Red Cross. My work during the American Civil War earned me the nickname "Angel of the Battlefield," and I continued to advocate for the rights of soldiers and civilians alike.

Who am I?

10. I was a civil rights activist and leader in the civil rights movement, best known for refusing to give up my seat on a segregated bus in Montgomery, Alabama. This act of defiance became a pivotal moment in the struggle for racial equality.

Who am I?

Answers: Who Am I? - American Historical Figures

1. Benjamin Franklin

Did you know? Benjamin Franklin is also known for his wit and writings, including "Poor Richard's Almanack," and his famous kite experiment to study electricity.

2. Frederick Douglass

Did you know? Frederick Douglass was a skilled orator and influential newspaper editor, advocating for the abolition of slavery and civil rights for all.

3. Susan B. Anthony

Did you know? Susan B. Anthony was arrested for voting illegally in the 1872 presidential election and became a symbol of the fight for women's suffrage.

4. Davy Crockett

Did you know? Davy Crockett was killed at the Battle of the Alamo and is remembered as a symbol of rugged American individualism and frontier spirit.

5. Andrew Carnegie

Did you know? Andrew Carnegie wrote "The Gospel of Wealth," advocating that the rich have a moral obligation to distribute their wealth for the public good.

6. Thomas Edison

Did you know? Thomas Edison held over 1,000 patents and was involved in the development of major technologies, including the motion picture camera and the alkaline storage battery.

7. Booker T. Washington

Did you know? Booker T. Washington was the first African American invited to the White House, where he dined with President Theodore Roosevelt.

8. Amelia Earhart

Did you know? Amelia Earhart was also a women's rights advocate and a member of the National Women's Party, fighting for gender equality in aviation and beyond.

9. Clara Barton

Did you know? Clara Barton worked tirelessly to locate missing soldiers and was instrumental in identifying thousands of unknown soldiers' graves after the Civil War.

10. Rosa Parks

Did you know? Rosa Parks' act of defiance in 1955 sparked the Montgomery Bus Boycott, a pivotal event in the American civil rights movement led by Martin Luther King Jr.

Who Am I?

Infamous Serial Killers

1. I was known as the "Killer Clown," often performing at children's parties and community events. However, behind the painted smile, I was responsible for the deaths of at least 33 young men.

Who am I?

2. My murders were linked to a series of cryptic letters sent to the police, each one taunting their efforts to capture me. Despite numerous suspects, my true identity remains unknown.

Who am I?

3. I lured young women to their deaths by pretending to be injured and asking for their help. My charm and good looks made it easy for me to gain their trust.

Who am I?

4. My case is one of the most gruesome in history, involving acts of cannibalism and necrophilia. I preyed on young men, often luring them back to my apartment.

Who am I?

5. I terrorized London in the late 1800s, brutally murdering women in the Whitechapel district. My identity has been the subject of speculation and numerous theories.

Who am I?

6. I convinced my followers that I was a messianic figure and led them to commit a series of brutal murders in 1969, believing it would spark an apocalyptic race war.

Who am I?

7. I was a nurse who took advantage of my position to kill my patients, often injecting them with lethal doses of drugs. My nickname is synonymous with "Angel of Death."

Who am I?

8. I was a member of a satanic cult and committed a series of ritualistic murders in California. My crimes were brutal and left a lasting impact on the community.

Who am I?

9. I targeted young boys, luring them away with promises of money or jobs, only to kill them and bury them in my crawl space.

Who am I?

10. I was a doctor who used my medical knowledge to kill, often experimenting on my victims. My case is one of the earliest recorded instances of a serial killer.

Who am I?

Answers: Who am I? - Infamous Serial Killers

1. John Wayne Gacy

Did you know? John Wayne Gacy's clown persona was known as "Pogo the Clown," and he performed at local parties and charity events. Gacy's final meal before his execution included fried chicken, fried shrimp, french fries, and a pound of strawberries.

2. The Zodiac Killer

Did you know? The Zodiac Killer's letters included a 408-symbol cryptogram, which was cracked by a high school teacher and his wife. Despite numerous suspects and ongoing investigations, the true identity of the Zodiac Killer remains one of the most infamous unsolved mysteries in criminal history.

3. Ted Bundy

Did you know? Ted Bundy once escaped from prison by jumping out of a library window and lived as a fugitive for several weeks. He was captured again after being on the FBI's Ten Most Wanted list and ultimately executed in the electric chair in 1989.

4. Jeffrey Dahmer

Did you know? Jeffrey Dahmer's first murder occurred just three weeks after his high school graduation. He was known to keep body parts of his victims as trophies and was killed by a fellow inmate in prison in 1994.

5. Jack the Ripper

Did you know? Despite numerous theories, the true identity of Jack the Ripper has never been confirmed. The killer's modus operandi included brutally mutilating his victims, leading to widespread fear and sensational newspaper coverage in Victorian London.

6. Charles Manson

Did you know? Charles Manson never actually committed any of the murders himself but orchestrated them through his followers, known as the "Manson Family." He believed that the murders would spark an apocalyptic race war he called "Helter Skelter," inspired by The Beatles' song.

7. Harold Shipman

Did you know? Harold Shipman is believed to be the most prolific serial killer in modern history, with estimates of his victims ranging from 200 to 250. He used his position as a general practitioner to administer lethal doses of painkillers to his patients.

8. Richard Ramirez

Did you know? Richard Ramirez, known as the "Night Stalker," was influenced by Satanism and often left pentagrams at his crime scenes. He was captured after being recognized and subdued by residents in an East Los Angeles neighborhood.

9. Dean Corll

Did you know? Dean Corll, known as the "Candy Man," lured young boys with candy from his family's factory before torturing and murdering them. He had two teenage accomplices who helped him abduct the victims.

10. H.H. Holmes

Did you know? H.H. Holmes built a hotel in Chicago, often referred to as the "Murder Castle," which was equipped with secret passages, trap doors, and soundproof rooms to carry out his murders. He confessed to

27 murders, though the actual number of his victims is believed to be much higher.

Who Am I?

World Leaders (2000s-Present)

Round 1: Easy

1. I was the 44th President of the United States and the first African American to hold the office. I won the Nobel Peace Prize in 2009 and am known for my "Yes We Can" campaign slogan.

Who am I?

2. I have been the Chancellor of Germany since 2005 and am known for my pragmatic and steady leadership. I grew up in East Germany and hold a doctorate in quantum chemistry.

Who am I?

3. I am the Prime Minister of Canada, known for my charismatic personality and progressive policies. My father also served as Prime Minister, and I am often seen sporting colorful socks.

Who am I?

4. I am the President of Russia, having held power as either President or Prime Minister since 1999. I am known for my strongman image, love of judo, and shirtless photo ops.

Who am I?

5. I am the former Prime Minister of the United Kingdom who led the country during the Brexit referendum. My tenure was marked by efforts to renegotiate the UK's relationship with the EU.

Who am I?

Round 2: Medium

6. I served as the President of France from 2017. I was a former investment banker and minister of the economy before founding a centrist political movement. I am known for my pro-European Union stance and attempts at economic reform.

Who am I?

7. I was the President of Brazil from 2003 to 2011 and was reelected in 2023. I am a former union leader and have been celebrated for reducing poverty but criticized for corruption scandals during my tenure.

Who am I?

8. I am the Prime Minister of India, known for my economic reforms and strong nationalist stance. I was the Chief Minister of Gujarat before becoming the head of the Indian government in 2014.

Who am I?

9. I served as the Prime Minister of the United Kingdom from 1997 to 2007. I was a key figure in the "New Labour" movement and played a significant role in the Northern Ireland peace process and the Iraq War.

Who am I?

10. I am the current President of China, having consolidated power and abolished term limits. My policies are known as the "Chinese Dream," and I have a significant influence on global affairs.

Who am I?

Round 3: Hard

11. I am the Supreme Leader of North Korea, having succeeded my father in 2011. My regime is known for its oppressive policies, nuclear ambitions, and isolationist stance.

Who am I?

12. I am the President of Ukraine, a former comedian and actor who played the president on television before being elected in 2019. My leadership has been tested by conflicts with Russia.

Who am I?

13. I have served as the Prime Minister of Singapore since 2004. My leadership is marked by a focus on economic growth, strict governance, and maintaining Singapore's status as a global financial hub.

Who am I?

14. I served as the President of the United States from 2001 to 2009. My presidency was defined by the response to the 9/11 attacks and the subsequent wars in Afghanistan and Iraq.

Who am I?

15. I am the current President of the Philippines, known for my controversial "War on Drugs" and outspoken, often inflammatory, rhetoric. I served as mayor of Davao City for over two decades before becoming President.

Who am I?

Answers: Who Am I? - World Leaders (2000s-Present)

1. **Barack Obama**

Did you know? Barack Obama is a big fan of comic books and has a collection of Spider-Man and Conan the Barbarian comics.

2. Angela Merkel

Did you know? Angela Merkel has been nicknamed "Mutti" (Mom) in Germany due to her maternal leadership style.

3. Justin Trudeau

Did you know? Justin Trudeau once worked as a snowboard instructor before entering politics.

4. Vladimir Putin

Did you know? Vladimir Putin is a black belt in judo and has authored a book on the sport.

5. David Cameron

Did you know? David Cameron is a descendant of King William IV, making him a distant relative of Queen Elizabeth II.

6. Emmanuel Macron

Did you know? Emmanuel Macron married his high school teacher, Brigitte Trogneux, who is 24 years his senior.

7. Luiz Inácio Lula da Silva

Did you know? Lula da Silva lost a finger in a factory accident when he was a metalworker before becoming a union leader.

8. Narendra Modi

Did you know? Narendra Modi was once a tea seller at a railway station before rising through the ranks of the BJP.

9. Tony Blair

Did you know? Tony Blair played guitar in a rock band called Ugly Rumours while he was a student at Oxford University.

10. Xi Jinping

Did you know? Xi Jinping's father was a revolutionary hero and a vice premier, but he fell out of favor during the Cultural Revolution.

11. Kim Jong-un

Did you know? Kim Jong-un studied in Switzerland under a false identity before becoming the leader of North Korea.

12. Volodymyr Zelensky

Did you know? Volodymyr Zelensky voiced the character of Paddington Bear in the Ukrainian dub of the animated film.

13. Lee Hsien Loong

Did you know? Lee Hsien Loong is the son of Singapore's founding Prime Minister, Lee Kuan Yew.

14. George W. Bush

Did you know? George W. Bush is an accomplished painter, focusing on portraits of world leaders and military personnel.

15. Rodrigo Duterte

Did you know? Rodrigo Duterte has openly admitted to personally killing criminal suspects when he was mayor of Davao City.

Who Am I?

Ancient Era (Prehistoric Era pre-600 B.C.E.)

Round 1: Easy

1. I am a legendary figure from ancient Mesopotamian mythology, known as the king of Uruk. My epic, named after me, is one of the

earliest works of literature in human history. My adventures include a quest for immortality and friendship with Enkidu.

Who am I?

2. I am an ancient Egyptian pharaoh, often considered one of the greatest and most powerful of the New Kingdom. I built many colossal statues and monuments, including Abu Simbel. My reign is frequently associated with the biblical Exodus.

Who am I?

3. I am the founder of the Persian Empire and known for my respectful treatment of the cultures and religions of the lands I conquered. My most famous decree, inscribed on a clay cylinder, is considered one of the first declarations of human rights.

Who am I?

4. I am an ancient Sumerian king, known for creating one of the world's earliest law codes. My code covered aspects of daily life and is famous for its principle of "an eye for an eye."

Who am I?

5. I am a semi-legendary lawgiver of ancient Sparta. I reformed the Spartan society and military, creating the strict and disciplined way of life that Sparta is known for.

Who am I?

Round 2: Medium

6. I am an ancient Chinese philosopher and politician, whose teachings and philosophy deeply influenced Chinese culture and society. My ideas are compiled in a collection called the "Analects."

Who am I?

7. I am a legendary figure from ancient Crete, known for the labyrinth and the Minotaur. My name is often associated with the earliest known European civilization, named after me.

Who am I?

8. I am a renowned female pharaoh of ancient Egypt, known for my prosperous and peaceful reign. I built a magnificent mortuary temple at Deir el-Bahri and often depicted myself with a false beard.

Who am I?

9. I am an ancient Indian prince who founded Buddhism. After attaining enlightenment, I shared my teachings, which include the Four Noble Truths and the Eightfold Path.

Who am I?

10. I am an ancient Greek poet, traditionally said to be the author of the epic poems "The Iliad" and "The Odyssey." My works are foundational texts of Western literature.

Who am I?

Round 3: Hard

11. I am a legendary king of the Akkadian Empire, often credited with founding the first known empire in history. My empire included much of Mesopotamia and parts of the Levant and Anatolia.

Who am I?

12. I am an ancient Egyptian pharaoh from the Old Kingdom, famous for commissioning the Great Pyramid of Giza, one of the Seven Wonders of the Ancient World.

Who am I?

13. I am an early king of the Assyrian Empire, known for my extensive building projects and military campaigns. My capital was Nineveh, which became a major cultural and economic center.

Who am I?

14. I am an ancient Chinese ruler from the Shang Dynasty, often considered the first historically verified Chinese dynasty. My reign included the development of writing, bronze casting, and urban planning.

Who am I?

15. I am a mythical king from ancient Greece, best known for my role in the Trojan War and my long journey home, which was famously recounted by Homer.

Who am I?

Round 4: Expert

16. I am an ancient Egyptian queen and the wife of Akhenaten. My bust is one of the most famous and admired works of ancient Egyptian art. I played a significant role in the religious revolution that temporarily replaced the traditional Egyptian pantheon with the worship of Aten.

Who am I?

17. I am an ancient Babylonian king, known for rebuilding Babylon and constructing the famous Hanging Gardens, one of the Seven Wonders of the Ancient World. My reign marked the height of the Neo-Babylonian Empire.

Who am I?

18. I am an ancient king of Lydia, famous for my immense wealth and the saying "as rich as Croesus." I reigned during the 6th century B.C.E. and was known for issuing the first true gold coins.

Who am I?

19. I am a legendary Greek hero, known for my strength and for performing twelve nearly impossible labors. My adventures include slaying the Nemean Lion and capturing the Golden Hind.

Who am I?

20. I am an ancient Mesopotamian goddess of love, beauty, sex, and war. I was worshipped in Sumer and Akkad and later became associated with the goddess Ishtar in Babylonian mythology.

Who am I?

Answers: Who Am I? - Ancient Era (Prehistoric Era pre-600 B.C.E.)

1. Gilgamesh

Did you know? The Epic of Gilgamesh is considered one of the earliest great works of literature, predating even the Iliad and the Odyssey.

2. Ramses II

Did you know? Ramses II lived to be around 90 years old, an impressive age for his time, and had over 200 children.

3. Cyrus the Great

Did you know? The Cyrus Cylinder is often considered the first charter of human rights, highlighting Cyrus's respect for the customs and religions of the lands he conquered.

4. Hammurabi

Did you know? Hammurabi's Code is one of the oldest deciphered writings of significant length in the world, containing 282 laws.

5. Lycurgus

Did you know? Lycurgus's reforms included the creation of the agoge, a rigorous education and training program mandated for all male Spartan citizens.

6. Confucius

Did you know? Confucius's teachings emphasized personal and governmental morality, correctness of social relationships, justice, and sincerity.

7. Minos

Did you know? The civilization named after King Minos, the Minoan civilization, is one of the earliest known in Europe and is famous for its advanced architecture and art.

8. Hatshepsut

Did you know? Hatshepsut often portrayed herself as a male pharaoh, complete with a false beard, to assert her authority.

9. Siddhartha Gautama (Buddha)

Did you know? After achieving enlightenment, Siddhartha Gautama spent the rest of his life teaching others how to achieve liberation from suffering.

10. Homer

Did you know? There is debate among scholars about whether Homer was a single individual or a collection of storytellers who contributed to the epics attributed to him.

11. Sargon of Akkad

Did you know? Sargon of Akkad's empire is considered the first known empire in history, establishing the pattern for future Mesopotamian empires.

12. Khufu (Cheops)

Did you know? The Great Pyramid of Giza, built for Khufu, was the tallest man-made structure in the world for over 3,800 years.

13. Ashurbanipal

Did you know? Ashurbanipal established the first systematically organized library in the ancient Middle East, the Library of Ashurbanipal in Nineveh.

14. Tang of Shang

Did you know? Tang of Shang is credited with overthrowing the tyrannical rule of the Xia dynasty, leading to the establishment of the Shang dynasty.

15. Odysseus

Did you know? Odysseus's journey home from the Trojan War, as recounted in the Odyssey, took ten years and involved numerous trials and adventures.

16. Nefertiti

Did you know? Nefertiti's name means "the beautiful one has come," and she was a key figure in the religious revolution led by her husband, Akhenaten.

17. Nebuchadnezzar II

Did you know? Nebuchadnezzar II's construction of the Hanging Gardens of Babylon is considered one of the Seven Wonders of the Ancient World, although their existence remains debated.

18. Croesus

Did you know? Croesus is credited with issuing the first true gold coins that were of a standard weight and purity, revolutionizing trade and commerce.

19. Heracles (Hercules)

Did you know? Heracles's twelve labors were penance for killing his wife and children in a fit of madness sent by Hera, the wife of Zeus.

20. Inanna (Ishtar)

Did you know? Inanna is one of the earliest deities whose stories include themes of love and war, and she was worshipped in temples across Mesopotamia.

Who Am I?

Classical Era to Middle Ages (600 B.C.E. to 1500 C.E.)

Round 1: Easy

1. I was a famous Greek philosopher who taught Aristotle and was a student of Socrates. My writings, such as "The Republic," explore justice, the ideal state, and the philosopher-king.

Who am I?

2. I was the first emperor of Rome, initiating the Pax Romana. My rule marked the end of the Roman Republic and the beginning of the Roman Empire.

Who am I?

3. I was the queen of the Ptolemaic Kingdom of Egypt and the last active ruler of the Egyptian Empire. My romantic liaisons with Julius Caesar and Mark Antony are legendary.

Who am I?

4. I was a Carthaginian general known for my tactical genius during the Second Punic War, famously crossing the Alps with war elephants to invade Italy.

Who am I?

5. I was the founder of Buddhism, attaining enlightenment under the Bodhi tree. My teachings include the Four Noble Truths and the Eightfold Path.

Who am I?

Round 2: Medium

6. I was a famous Greek mathematician and inventor from Syracuse. Known for my work in geometry and mechanics, I famously exclaimed "Eureka!" upon discovering the principle of buoyancy.

Who am I?

7. I was the Roman gladiator who led a major slave uprising against the Roman Republic, known as the Third Servile War.

Who am I?

8. I was a Byzantine emperor known for my comprehensive codification of Roman law, known as "Corpus Juris Civilis," which influenced the legal systems of many modern European nations.

Who am I?

9. I was the king of the Franks and Lombards, crowned Emperor of the Romans in 800 C.E., and known as the "Father of Europe." My reign marked the Carolingian Renaissance.

Who am I?

10. I was the Viking leader who became the first Norman King of England after winning the Battle of Hastings in 1066.

Who am I?

Round 3: Hard

11. I was the Macedonian king who created one of the largest empires in history by the age of 30, spreading Greek culture throughout the known world. My tutor was Aristotle.

Who am I?

12. I was the Persian king who expanded the Achaemenid Empire to its greatest extent, creating a multi-ethnic empire known for its tolerance and administrative innovations.

Who am I?

13. I was a medieval king of England, known for signing the Magna Carta in 1215, which limited royal power and laid the foundation for modern parliamentary democracy.

Who am I?

14. I was a Chinese philosopher whose teachings on ethics, family loyalty, and social harmony deeply influenced Chinese culture. My thoughts are recorded in the "Analects."

Who am I?

15. I was the founder of the Mongol Empire, the largest contiguous empire in history. My conquests stretched from East Asia to Europe, and I established a code of laws known as the Yassa.

Who am I?

Round 4: Expert

16. I was the Athenian statesman who led Athens during its Golden Age, transforming it into an empire and overseeing the construction of the Parthenon.

Who am I?

17. I was a Muslim scholar and traveler who documented my extensive travels across the Islamic world and beyond in my work, "Rihla" (The Journey).

Who am I?

18. I was the Frankish king who defended Western Europe from Muslim invasions, most notably at the Battle of Tours in 732 C.E., halting the advance of Islam into Europe.

Who am I?

19. I was an English philosopher and friar who advocated for the empirical method and made significant contributions to the development of modern science during the medieval period.

Who am I?

20. I was the Queen of the Iceni tribe who led a major uprising against the occupying Roman forces in Britain around 60-61 C.E.

Who am I?

Answers: Who Am I? - Classical Era to Middle Ages (600 B.C.E. to 1500 C.E.)

1. **Plato**

Did you know? Plato founded the Academy in Athens, one of the earliest institutions of higher learning in the Western world.

2. **Augustus (Octavian)**

Did you know? Augustus established the Praetorian Guard, a special force of bodyguards used by Roman Emperors.

3. **Cleopatra VII**

Did you know? Cleopatra could speak several languages and was one of the few members of her dynasty to learn Egyptian.

4. Hannibal Barca

Did you know? Hannibal's crossing of the Alps with war elephants remains one of the most remarkable military feats in history.

5. Siddhartha Gautama (Buddha)

Did you know? Buddha's teachings spread rapidly throughout Asia, profoundly influencing many cultures and societies.

6. Archimedes

Did you know? Archimedes invented the Archimedes screw, a device used for raising water, which is still in use today.

7. Spartacus

Did you know? Spartacus's rebellion posed such a threat to Rome that they sent multiple legions to suppress it.

8. Justinian I

Did you know? Justinian I also initiated an ambitious building program, including the reconstruction of the Hagia Sophia.

9. Charlemagne

Did you know? Charlemagne's reign encouraged the Carolingian Renaissance, a revival of art, religion, and culture through the Catholic Church.

10. William the Conqueror

Did you know? William the Conqueror commissioned the Domesday Book, a great survey of his English lands and possessions.

11. Alexander the Great

Did you know? Alexander the Great never lost a battle during his 15 years of conquest.

12. Darius the Great

Did you know? Darius the Great built the famous Royal Road, which facilitated rapid communication and trade across the empire.

13. King John

Did you know? King John's misrule and heavy taxation led to the rebellion of his barons and the eventual signing of the Magna Carta.

14. Confucius

Did you know? Confucius's real name was Kong Qiu, and he is often referred to as "Master Kong" in China.

15. Genghis Khan

Did you know? Genghis Khan's birth name was Temujin, and he united the Mongol tribes under his rule before embarking on his conquests.

16. Pericles

Did you know? Pericles's Funeral Oration is one of the most famous speeches in ancient history, praising the democratic values of Athens.

17. Ibn Battuta

Did you know? Ibn Battuta traveled over 75,000 miles, visiting nearly every Muslim country of his time and beyond.

18. Charles Martel

Did you know? Charles Martel's victory at the Battle of Tours is often credited with preserving Christianity as the dominant faith in Europe.

19. Roger Bacon

Did you know? Roger Bacon was one of the earliest European advocates of the scientific method, emphasizing observation and experimentation.

20. Boudica

Did you know? Boudica's revolt led to the destruction of several Roman settlements, including present-day London, before her defeat.

Who Am I?

Age of Exploration to Pre-World War I (1500-1914)

Round 1: Easy

1. I was the Queen of England from 1558 to 1603, known for defeating the Spanish Armada and fostering the English Renaissance. My reign is often referred to as the "Golden Age."

Who am I?

2. I was a French military leader who rose to prominence during the French Revolution and became Emperor of the French. I established the Napoleonic Code and my defeat at Waterloo ended my rule.

Who am I?

3. I was the first President of the United States and led the American Revolutionary War against Britain. My face is famously depicted on the one-dollar bill.

Who am I?

4. I was an Italian explorer who completed four voyages across the Atlantic Ocean, opening the way for the widespread European exploration and colonization of the Americas. I sailed under the Spanish flag.

Who am I?

5. I was a German composer and pianist, known for my symphonies, sonatas, and concertos. I continued to compose even after becoming completely deaf.

Who am I?

Round 2: Medium

6. I was the czar of Russia who modernized and expanded the Russian Empire. I founded the city of St. Petersburg and established it as Russia's new capital in 1703.

Who am I?

7. I was an Italian polymath of the Renaissance who painted the "Mona Lisa" and "The Last Supper." I was also an accomplished inventor, scientist, and anatomist.

Who am I?

8. I was the founder of the Qing dynasty in China, which was the last imperial dynasty of China. My reign saw significant territorial expansion and the consolidation of Manchu rule.

Who am I?

9. I was the English naturalist who developed the theory of evolution by natural selection, published in my book "On the Origin of Species."

Who am I?

10. I was a military and political leader in South America who played a key role in the independence movements of several Latin American countries from Spanish rule, earning me the nickname "The Liberator."

Who am I?

Round 3: Hard

11. I was the Emperor of Ethiopia who successfully resisted European colonization by defeating the Italian army at the Battle of Adwa in 1896.

Who am I?

12. I was a German philosopher known for my works on existentialism and the concept of the "Übermensch." I famously declared that "God is dead" in my work "Thus Spoke Zarathustra."

Who am I?

13. I was an influential abolitionist and writer, known for my speeches against slavery and my autobiography detailing my life as a former slave in the United States.

Who am I?

14. I was a British queen who reigned from 1837 to 1901, overseeing the expansion of the British Empire and a period of industrial, cultural, and scientific advancement known as the Victorian era.

Who am I?

15. I was a Haitian general who led the Haitian Revolution against French colonial rule, ultimately establishing Haiti as the first independent black republic in 1804.

Who am I?

Round 4: Expert

16. I was a Japanese emperor whose reign, known as the Meiji Restoration, transformed Japan from a feudal society into a modern industrialized nation.

Who am I?

17. I was an Italian nationalist and revolutionary who played a key role in the unification of Italy. I led the Expedition of the Thousand in 1860, which contributed to the establishment of the Kingdom of Italy.

Who am I?

18. I was a Prussian statesman who unified Germany in 1871 and served as its first Chancellor. My foreign policy is often summarized by the phrase "blood and iron."

Who am I?

19. I was an Austrian neurologist and the founder of psychoanalysis. My theories on the unconscious mind and the interpretation of dreams have had a profound impact on psychology and psychiatry.

Who am I?

20. I was the last monarch of the Kingdom of Hawaii before it was annexed by the United States in 1898. My reign was marked by efforts to resist the increasing influence of American settlers.

Who am I?

Answers: Who Am I? - Age of Exploration to Pre-World War I (1500-1914)

1. Elizabeth I

Did you know? Elizabeth I was known as the "Virgin Queen" because she never married, and Virginia in the United States is named in her honor.

2. Napoleon Bonaparte

Did you know? Napoleon was exiled twice, first to the island of Elba and then to the island of Saint Helena, where he died.

3. George Washington

Did you know? George Washington was unanimously elected as the first President of the United States by the Electoral College.

4. Christopher Columbus

Did you know? Christopher Columbus's voyages were funded by King Ferdinand and Queen Isabella of Spain.

5. Ludwig van Beethoven

Did you know? Beethoven's Ninth Symphony, which includes the famous "Ode to Joy," was composed after he had become completely deaf.

6. Peter the Great

Did you know? Peter the Great traveled incognito across Europe to learn about shipbuilding and other trades to modernize Russia.

7. Leonardo da Vinci

Did you know? Leonardo da Vinci wrote his notes in mirror writing, which can only be read correctly when held up to a mirror.

8. Nurhaci

Did you know? Nurhaci initiated the rise of the Qing dynasty by unifying the Jurchen tribes and rebelling against the Ming dynasty.

9. Charles Darwin

Did you know? Charles Darwin's voyage on the HMS Beagle lasted five years and provided much of the evidence for his theory of evolution.

10. Simón Bolívar

Did you know? Simón Bolívar is often referred to as the "George Washington of South America" for his role in the continent's independence movements.

11. Menelik II

Did you know? Menelik II's victory at the Battle of Adwa ensured Ethiopia's sovereignty and made it the only African country to successfully resist European colonization during the Scramble for Africa.

12. Friedrich Nietzsche

Did you know? Friedrich Nietzsche's ideas were later co-opted and misinterpreted by various political movements, including the Nazis, despite Nietzsche's disdain for nationalism and anti-Semitism.

13. Frederick Douglass

Did you know? Frederick Douglass was the first African American nominated for Vice President of the United States as Victoria Woodhull's running mate in 1872.

14. Queen Victoria

Did you know? Queen Victoria was the longest-reigning British monarch until she was surpassed by Queen Elizabeth II in 2015.

15. Toussaint L'Ouverture

Did you know? Toussaint L'Ouverture was captured by the French and died in a prison in France before Haiti achieved full independence.

16. Emperor Meiji

Did you know? The Meiji Restoration led to the abolition of the samurai class and the adoption of Western-style military and industrial practices in Japan.

17. Giuseppe Garibaldi

Did you know? Giuseppe Garibaldi's followers were known as the "Redshirts" due to the color of their uniforms.

18. Otto von Bismarck

Did you know? Otto von Bismarck is credited with the phrase "The great questions of the day will not be settled by speeches and majority decisions but by iron and blood."

19. Sigmund Freud

Did you know? Sigmund Freud's early work on cocaine and its potential uses in medical treatments became controversial and was later abandoned.

20. Queen Lili'uokalani

Did you know? Queen Lili'uokalani was an accomplished musician and composed the famous Hawaiian song "Aloha 'Oe."

Who Am I?

Between the Wars and World War II (1914-1945)

Round 1: Easy

1. I was the 32nd President of the United States, serving four terms from 1933 to 1945. I led the country through the Great Depression and World War II, and my New Deal policies aimed to restore economic stability.

Who am I?

2. I was the leader of the Soviet Union from 1924 until my death in 1953. My reign was marked by widespread purges, forced labor camps, and a significant role in World War II.

Who am I?

3. I was the fascist dictator of Italy from 1922 to 1943. I founded the National Fascist Party and was known as "Il Duce." My alliance with Nazi Germany led to Italy's involvement in World War II.

Who am I?

4. I was the Emperor of Japan from 1926 to 1989. My reign saw Japan's militarization, involvement in World War II, and subsequent occupation and reconstruction by Allied forces.

Who am I?

5. I was a British writer and the author of "1984" and "Animal Farm," which critiqued totalitarian regimes. My real name was Eric Arthur Blair.

Who am I?

Round 2: Medium

6. I was the leader of the Chinese Nationalist Party (Kuomintang) and a key figure in the fight against Japanese invasion during World War II. I later fled to Taiwan after losing the Chinese Civil War.

Who am I?

7. I was an American aviator and the first person to fly solo nonstop across the Atlantic Ocean in 1927. My plane was called the Spirit of St. Louis.

Who am I?

8. I was a pioneering British economist whose ideas fundamentally changed the theory and practice of macroeconomics and economic policies. My work during the Great Depression influenced many governments' responses.

Who am I?

9. I was an Indian nationalist leader who led the struggle for independence from British rule through nonviolent resistance. I was assassinated in 1948.

Who am I?

10. I was the first woman to fly solo across the Atlantic Ocean. I disappeared in 1937 while attempting to circumnavigate the globe.

Who am I?

Round 3: Hard

11. I was the founder of modern Turkey and its first President. I implemented extensive reforms to secularize and westernize the country.

Who am I?

12. I was a Norwegian explorer known for my polar expeditions. I was the first person to reach both the North and South Poles.

Who am I?

13 I was an influential Mexican artist known for my self-portraits and works inspired by nature and Mexican artifacts. I was married to Diego Rivera.

Who am I?

14. I was a Spanish general who led the Nationalist forces to victory in the Spanish Civil War, subsequently ruling Spain as a dictator until my death in 1975.

Who am I?

15. I was an American actress and singer known as "The First Lady of Song." My career spanned six decades, and I was known for my purity of tone and impeccable diction.

Who am I?

Answers: Who Am I? - Between the Wars and World War II (1914-1945)

1. **Franklin D. Roosevelt**

Did you know? Franklin D. Roosevelt was the only U.S. president to serve more than two terms, leading the country through some of its most challenging times.

2. **Joseph Stalin**

Did you know? Stalin's birth name was Ioseb Besarionis dze Jughashvili, and he adopted the name Stalin, meaning "man of steel," in the early 1900s.

3. Benito Mussolini

Did you know? Mussolini was originally a socialist before founding the Fascist Party, and he survived several assassination attempts.

4. Emperor Hirohito

Did you know? After Japan's surrender in World War II, Hirohito was allowed to remain emperor but was forced to renounce his divine status.

5. George Orwell

Did you know? George Orwell's experiences fighting in the Spanish Civil War greatly influenced his writing, particularly "Homage to Catalonia."

6. Chiang Kai-shek

Did you know? Chiang Kai-shek's wife, Soong Mei-ling, was a powerful figure in her own right and played a significant role in garnering American support during World War II.

7. Charles Lindbergh

Did you know? Charles Lindbergh's son was famously kidnapped and murdered in what was dubbed the "Crime of the Century."

8. John Maynard Keynes

Did you know? Keynes advocated for increased government expenditures and lower taxes to stimulate demand and pull the global economy out of the Great Depression.

9. Mahatma Gandhi

Did you know? Gandhi's philosophy of nonviolence and civil disobedience inspired future civil rights movements around the world, including Martin Luther King Jr.'s efforts in the United States.

10. Amelia Earhart

Did you know? Amelia Earhart's disappearance remains one of the greatest unsolved mysteries of the 20th century, with numerous theories about her fate.

11. Mustafa Kemal Atatürk

Did you know? Atatürk's reforms included abolishing the Ottoman Caliphate, introducing a new legal code, and replacing the Arabic script with the Latin alphabet for the Turkish language.

12. Roald Amundsen

Did you know? Roald Amundsen's successful South Pole expedition in 1911 was in direct competition with the British expedition led by Robert Falcon Scott.

13. Frida Kahlo

Did you know? Frida Kahlo's art was deeply personal and often included symbolic portrayals of physical and emotional pain, reflecting her lifelong health problems.

14. Francisco Franco

Did you know? Franco remained neutral during World War II, although he did send a volunteer unit to fight alongside the Germans on the Eastern Front against the Soviet Union.

15. Ella Fitzgerald

Did you know? Ella Fitzgerald won 13 Grammy Awards during her career, making her one of the most celebrated jazz singers in history.

What Film Am I?

IMDb's Top 30 Films - Famous Films

Round 1: Easy

1. I am a film about a man who is wrongfully imprisoned for decades. He maintains hope and forms a lasting friendship with another inmate. The story culminates in a dramatic escape and redemption. "Get busy living, or get busy dying."

What film am I?

2. I am a film about a powerful crime family in New York, focusing on the rise of Michael Corleone. My iconic scenes include a horse's head in a bed and the line, "I'm gonna make him an offer he can't refuse."

What film am I?

3. I am a film about a vigilante superhero facing off against his archenemy, the Joker, who creates chaos in Gotham City. Famous for my line, "Why so serious?"

What film am I?

4. I am a film that continues the saga of a powerful crime family, featuring the rise of Michael Corleone and flashbacks to Vito Corleone's early life in Sicily and New York. My story is both a sequel and a prequel.

What film am I?

5. I am a courtroom drama that revolves around twelve jurors deliberating the fate of a young man accused of murder. The story highlights the prejudices and biases of the jurors. "The burden of proof is on the prosecution."

What film am I?

Round 2: Medium

6. I am a film about a businessman who saves over a thousand Jewish refugees during the Holocaust by employing them in his factories. My film is shot primarily in black and white with a poignant use of color.

What film am I?

7. I am the final installment of an epic trilogy, where the forces of good battle against the dark lord Sauron. My story culminates in the destruction of the One Ring. "The age of men is over. The time of the Orc has come."

What film am I?

8. I am a film that intertwines multiple stories with nonlinear narratives. My characters include a hitman, a boxer, and a gangster's wife. "I said Goddamn! Goddamn."

What film am I?

9. I am the first part of an epic fantasy trilogy where a young hobbit sets out on a perilous journey to destroy a powerful ring. My companions include a wizard, an elf, a dwarf, and other hobbits. "One ring to rule them all."

What film am I?

10. I am a spaghetti western that follows three gunslingers competing to find a hidden treasure during the American Civil War. My soundtrack is iconic, and my final duel is legendary. "When you have to shoot, shoot. Don't talk."

What film am I?

Round 3: Hard

11. I am a film about a man with a low IQ who achieves extraordinary things in his life, from playing college football to fighting in Vietnam,

and starting a shrimp business. "Life is like a box of chocolates; you never know what you're gonna get."

What film am I?

12. I am a film about an insomniac office worker and a soap salesman who start an underground fight club. The first rule is, "You do not talk about Fight Club."

What film am I?

13. I am a film about a thief who enters people's dreams to steal secrets. My team is tasked with planting an idea in someone's mind, a process called "inception." "You mustn't be afraid to dream a little bigger, darling."

What film am I?

14. I am the second part of an epic fantasy trilogy where the fellowship is scattered, and the kingdoms of men face the threat of Sauron's army. My climax is the Battle of Helm's Deep. "The battle for Helm's Deep is over; the battle for Middle-earth is about to begin."

What film am I?

15. I am the second film in a famous space opera saga. I feature a shocking revelation about the protagonist's parentage and the struggle of the Rebel Alliance against the Galactic Empire. "I am your father."

What film am I?

Round 4: Expert

16. I am a film about a hacker who discovers that the reality he knows is a simulated reality created by intelligent machines. He joins a rebellion to free humanity. "There is no spoon."

What film am I?

17. I am a film about the rise and fall of three gangsters in the 1960s and 70s, based on a true story. My scenes include the famous tracking

shot through the Copacabana nightclub. "As far back as I can remember, I always wanted to be a gangster."

What film am I?

18. I am a film set in a mental institution where a rebellious patient challenges the oppressive rules of the head nurse. My protagonist's antics lead to a tragic conclusion. "It's as real as it gets, man."

What film am I?

19. I am a film about two detectives hunting a serial killer who uses the seven deadly sins as his motives. The climax reveals a horrifying twist. "What's in the box?"

What film am I?

20. I am a film about a man contemplating suicide on Christmas Eve and an angel who shows him how different the world would be without him. "Every time a bell rings, an angel gets his wings."

What film am I?

Round 5: Master

21. I am a film about a brilliant but manipulative psychiatrist who helps an FBI trainee track a serial killer. My protagonist's chilling voice is unforgettable. "I ate his liver with some fava beans and a nice Chianti."

What film am I?

22. I am a film about a mission to rescue a paratrooper behind enemy lines in World War II. My opening sequence depicts the brutal D-Day landing. "Earn this."

What film am I?

23. I am a Japanese animated film about a young girl who becomes trapped in a strange, magical world and must find a way to rescue her parents. "Welcome the rich man, he's hard for you to miss, his butt keeps getting bigger, so there's plenty there to kiss!"

What film am I?

24. I am a film set during the Holocaust, where a father uses humor and imagination to shield his son from the horrors around them. "This is a simple game. You throw the ball. You hit the ball. You catch the ball."

What film am I?

25. I am a film about a death row corrections officer who witnesses supernatural events following the arrival of a mysterious inmate with a miraculous gift. "I'm tired, boss. Tired of bein' on the road, lonely as a sparrow in the rain."

What film am I?

26. I am a science fiction film about a group of explorers who travel through a wormhole in search of a new habitable planet for humanity. "Do not go gentle into that good night."

What film am I?

27. I am the sequel to a groundbreaking sci-fi film about a cyborg sent back in time to protect a young boy who will become a future resistance leader. "Hasta la vista, baby."

What film am I?

28. I am a film about a teenager who travels back in time and inadvertently changes the course of his parents' lives. He must ensure they fall in love to return to his own time. "Great Scott!"

What film am I?

29. I am a film about a Polish-Jewish pianist who survives the Holocaust by hiding in the ruins of Warsaw. "I'm cold and hungry and, I have nowhere else to go."

What film am I?

30. I am a film about a young lion cub who must overcome his uncle Scar to reclaim his kingdom. My friends include a meerkat and a warthog who live by the motto "Hakuna Matata."

What film am I?

Answers: What Film Am I? - Famous Films

1. **The Shawshank Redemption**

Did you know? "The Shawshank Redemption" is based on a novella by Stephen King called "Rita Hayworth and Shawshank Redemption."

2. **The Godfather**

Did you know? "The Godfather" won three Academy Awards, including Best Picture, and is considered one of the greatest films in cinema history.

3. **The Dark Knight**

Did you know? Heath Ledger posthumously won the Academy Award for Best Supporting Actor for his role as the Joker.

4. **The Godfather: Part II**

Did you know? "The Godfather: Part II" is both a sequel and a prequel, continuing Michael Corleone's story while also exploring Vito Corleone's past.

5. **12 Angry Men**

Did you know? "12 Angry Men" was initially a television play before being adapted into a feature film directed by Sidney Lumet.

6. **Schindler's List**

Did you know? Steven Spielberg, the director, was initially reluctant to make the film and tried to pass the project to other directors.

7. **The Lord of the Rings: The Return of the King**

Did you know? "The Return of the King" won all 11 Academy Awards it was nominated for, including Best Picture.

8. **Pulp Fiction**

Did you know? "Pulp Fiction" won the Palme d'Or at the 1994 Cannes Film Festival and revitalized John Travolta's career.

9. The Lord of the Rings: The Fellowship of the Ring

Did you know? "The Fellowship of the Ring" features extensive use of New Zealand landscapes, which became iconic for the series.

10. The Good, the Bad and the Ugly

Did you know? Clint Eastwood was paid $250,000 for his role, making him the highest-paid actor for a spaghetti western at the time.

11. Forrest Gump

Did you know? Tom Hanks won his second consecutive Best Actor Oscar for his role in "Forrest Gump."

12. Fight Club

Did you know? "Fight Club" initially received mixed reviews but has since become a cult classic, especially among younger audiences.

13. Inception

Did you know? Director Christopher Nolan spent ten years writing the screenplay for "Inception."

14. The Lord of the Rings: The Two Towers

Did you know? The Battle of Helm's Deep took 120 days to film and involved hundreds of extras.

15. Star Wars: Episode V - The Empire Strikes Back

Did you know? "The Empire Strikes Back" is widely regarded as the best film in the Star Wars franchise and introduced the iconic line, "I am your father."

16. The Matrix

Did you know? The Wachowskis, the film's directors, required all principal actors to read philosophical texts and watch specific movies to understand the film's themes better.

17. Goodfellas

Did you know? "Goodfellas" is based on the non-fiction book "Wiseguy" by Nicholas Pileggi, who also co-wrote the screenplay with Martin Scorsese.

18. One Flew Over the Cuckoo's Nest

Did you know? Jack Nicholson's performance in "One Flew Over the Cuckoo's Nest" earned him his first Academy Award for Best Actor.

19. Se7en

Did you know? The ending of "Se7en" was almost changed by the studio, but director David Fincher and actor Brad Pitt insisted on keeping the original, darker conclusion.

20. It's a Wonderful Life

Did you know? "It's a Wonderful Life" was not initially successful at the box office but has since become a beloved Christmas classic.

21. The Silence of the Lambs

Did you know? "The Silence of the Lambs" won the "Big Five" Academy Awards: Best Picture, Best Director, Best Actor, Best Actress, and Best Adapted Screenplay.

22. Saving Private Ryan

Did you know? The D-Day landing scenes in "Saving Private Ryan" were so realistic that some veterans of the invasion were overwhelmed by watching them.

23. Spirited Away

Did you know? "Spirited Away" won the Academy Award for Best Animated Feature and is the highest-grossing film in Japanese history.

24. Life Is Beautiful

Did you know? Roberto Benigni, who starred in and directed "Life Is Beautiful," won the Oscar for Best Actor and famously climbed over chairs to reach the stage.

25. The Green Mile

Did you know? "The Green Mile" is based on a serialized novel by Stephen King and features a powerful performance by Michael Clarke Duncan as John Coffey.

26. Interstellar

Did you know? The black hole depicted in "Interstellar" is considered one of the most accurate portrayals of a black hole in film, based on calculations by physicist Kip Thorne.

27. Terminator 2: Judgment Day

Did you know? "Terminator 2: Judgment Day" was one of the most expensive films ever made at the time, with groundbreaking special effects.

28. Back to the Future

Did you know? Michael J. Fox filmed "Back to the Future" while still working on the TV show "Family Ties," often working on the movie at night.

29. The Pianist

Did you know? Adrien Brody won the Academy Award for Best Actor for his role in "The Pianist," and at 29, he was the youngest actor to win the award.

30. The Lion King

Did you know? "The Lion King" was the highest-grossing animated film of all time until it was surpassed by "Frozen" in 2013.

Who Am I?

Famous Music Artists (Top Grammy Winners)

Round 1: Easy

1. I am an American singer and actress known for my powerhouse vocals and hits that have become anthems. "I Will Always Love You" is one of my most famous songs, and I hold the record for the most Grammy Awards won in a single night by a female artist. Fun fact: I had a tumultuous marriage with Bobby Brown.

Who am I?

2. I am an English singer-songwriter and a member of one of the most famous bands in history. My songs often feature introspective lyrics like, "Hey Jude, don't make it bad." Fun fact: I was knighted by the Queen of England in 1997.

Who am I?

3. I am an American pop icon who started my career in a family band. My groundbreaking album, which includes "It's close to midnight, and something evil's lurking in the dark," revolutionized the music video industry. Fun fact: I had a pet chimpanzee named Bubbles.

Who am I?

4. I am a Canadian singer-songwriter known for my unique voice and introspective lyrics. One of my famous songs includes the line, "They paved paradise and put up a parking lot." Fun fact: I am also a celebrated painter.

Who am I?

5. I am an American jazz singer and pianist known for my smooth voice and timeless classics. My iconic song includes the lyrics, "Unforgettable, that's what you are." Fun fact: I was the first African American to host a television variety show.

Who am I?

Round 2: Medium

6. I am an American singer-songwriter whose lyrics often reflect social issues and political activism. One of my famous songs includes the line, "How many roads must a man walk down before you call him a man?" Fun fact: I won a Nobel Prize in Literature in 2016.

Who am I?

7. I am an American singer and songwriter known for my high-energy performances and catchy tunes. One of my songs includes the lyrics, "Don't believe me, just watch!" Fun fact: I can play multiple instruments, including the drums, guitar, and piano.

Who am I?

8. I am an American rock guitarist and singer known for my innovative style and electrifying performances. My famous song includes the lyrics, "Excuse me while I kiss the sky." Fun fact: I was left-handed but played a right-handed guitar upside down.

Who am I?

9. I am a British singer-songwriter known for my powerful voice and emotionally charged songs. One of my famous songs includes the lyrics, "We could have had it all, rolling in the deep." Fun fact: I once underwent throat surgery and made a successful comeback.

Who am I?

10. I am an American singer-songwriter and producer who has won multiple Grammys. One of my songs includes the lyrics, "Cause all of

me loves all of you." Fun fact: I graduated from the University of Pennsylvania with a degree in English.

Who am I?

Round 3: Hard

11. I am an American singer and actress known for my incredible vocal range and diva persona. My famous song includes the lyrics, "Cause we belong together now, yeah." Fun fact: I have a pet dog named Jack and a famous "Mimi" nickname.

Who am I?

12. I am a British singer-songwriter known for my eclectic style and theatrical performances. One of my famous songs includes the lyrics, "Is this the real life? Is this just fantasy?" Fun fact: I was born in Zanzibar and had a significant overbite.

Who am I?

13. I am an American singer-songwriter and producer known for my smooth, soulful voice. One of my famous songs includes the lyrics, "When I see your face, there's not a thing that I would change." Fun fact: I was discovered at a high school talent show.

Who am I?

14. I am a British singer-songwriter and guitarist known for my blues influence and masterful guitar skills. One of my famous songs includes the lyrics, "Layla, you got me on my knees." Fun fact: I am the only artist inducted into the Rock and Roll Hall of Fame three times.

Who am I?

15. I am an American singer-songwriter known for my pop hits and iconic fashion sense. One of my famous songs includes the lyrics, "Just dance, gonna be okay." Fun fact: I once wore a dress made entirely of meat to an awards show.

Who am I?

Answers: Who Am I? - Famous Music Artists (Top Grammy Winners)

1. **Whitney Houston**

Did you know? Whitney Houston's rendition of "The Star-Spangled Banner" at Super Bowl XXV became one of the best-selling singles of all time.

2. **Paul McCartney**

Did you know? Paul McCartney wrote "Yesterday," one of the most covered songs in the history of recorded music, after dreaming the melody.

3. **Michael Jackson**

Did you know? Michael Jackson's moonwalk dance move, first performed during "Billie Jean," became his signature move.

4. **Joni Mitchell**

Did you know? Joni Mitchell's album "Blue" is often cited as one of the greatest albums of all time.

5. **Nat King Cole**

Did you know? Nat King Cole's "The Christmas Song" ("Chestnuts Roasting on an Open Fire") is a holiday classic played every year.

6. **Bob Dylan**

Did you know? Bob Dylan's real name is Robert Zimmerman, and he took his stage name in honor of the poet Dylan Thomas.

7. **Bruno Mars**

Did you know? Bruno Mars's real name is Peter Gene Hernandez, and he got his stage name from the nickname "Bruno," given by his father.

8. **Jimi Hendrix**

Did you know? Jimi Hendrix was discharged from the U.S. Army for "unsuitability" after a year of service.

9. Adele

Did you know? Adele's album "21" became the best-selling album of the 21st century in the UK.

10. John Legend

Did you know? John Legend's birth name is John Roger Stephens, and he was given the nickname "Legend" by poet J. Ivy.

11. Mariah Carey

Did you know? Mariah Carey holds the record for the most number-one singles by a solo artist on the Billboard Hot 100 chart.

12. Freddie Mercury

Did you know? Freddie Mercury designed Queen's logo, known as the Queen Crest, which features the zodiac signs of the band members.

13. Bruno Mars

Did you know? Bruno Mars won his first Grammy Award for the hit song "Just the Way You Are."

14. Eric Clapton

Did you know? Eric Clapton's nickname is "Slowhand," and he is known for his extensive work with bands like Cream and The Yardbirds.

15. Lady Gaga

Did you know? Lady Gaga's real name is Stefani Joanne Angelina Germanotta, and she started playing the piano at the age of four.

Who Am I?

Famous Authors

Round 1: Easy

1. I am an English playwright and poet, renowned for my works "Hamlet," "Romeo and Juliet," and "Macbeth." My Globe Theatre was a hub of entertainment in London.

Who am I?

2. I am an ancient Greek poet, traditionally said to be the author of the epic poems "The Iliad" and "The Odyssey." My works explore themes of heroism and adventure.

Who am I?

3. I am a Russian novelist best known for my epic novels "War and Peace" and "Anna Karenina." My exploration of human nature and society has made me a literary giant.

Who am I?

4. I am an English novelist known for my sharp social commentary and beloved works "Pride and Prejudice" and "Sense and Sensibility." My keen observations of manners and marriage remain popular today.

Who am I?

5. I am an English writer and social critic, famous for "A Tale of Two Cities" and "Great Expectations." My vivid characters and depictions of Victorian life are unforgettable.

Who am I?

Round 2: Medium

6. I am an American author known for my witty and satirical novels "The Adventures of Tom Sawyer" and "Adventures of Huckleberry Finn." My real name is Samuel Clemens.

Who am I?

7. I am an Irish novelist and short story writer, best known for my stream-of-consciousness masterpiece "Ulysses" and the collection "Dubliners." My work often focuses on the life of Dublin.

Who am I?

8. I am a Russian novelist, famous for exploring psychological depth in "Crime and Punishment" and "The Brothers Karamazov." My works delve into the complexities of faith and doubt.

Who am I?

9. I am a Colombian novelist known for my magical realism, particularly in "One Hundred Years of Solitude" and "Love in the Time of Cholera." My stories weave the fantastical with the mundane.

Who am I?

10. I am an American poet known for my reclusive life and posthumously published poetry. My short, enigmatic verses often explore themes of death and immortality.

Who am I?

Round 3: Hard

11. I am an American writer and Nobel Prize laureate, known for my complex narratives in "The Sound and the Fury." My fictional Yoknapatawpha County is a microcosm of Southern life.

Who am I?

12. I am an English writer known for my modernist novels "Mrs. Dalloway" and "To the Lighthouse." My use of stream-of-consciousness has influenced countless writers.

Who am I?

13. I am an Argentine writer known for my intricate and surreal short stories. My works, such as those in "Ficciones," often explore labyrinths and mirrors.

Who am I?

14. I am an American novelist and short story writer, known for my sparse prose and works like "The Old Man and the Sea" and "A Farewell to Arms." My life mirrored the adventurous spirit of my characters.

Who am I?

15. I am an American-British poet, essayist, and playwright, known for my landmark poems "The Waste Land" and "Four Quartets." My work revolutionized modernist poetry.

Who am I?

Round 4: Expert

16. I am an English novelist and essayist, famous for my dystopian works "1984" and "Animal Farm." My real name was Eric Arthur Blair.

Who am I?

17. I am a German-speaking Bohemian writer known for my nightmarish and surreal stories, including "The Metamorphosis" and "The Trial." My works often depict oppressive bureaucracies.

Who am I?

18. I am an American writer, poet, and literary critic, known for my dark and macabre tales like "The Raven" and "The Tell-Tale Heart." My troubled life fueled my gothic imagination.

Who am I?

19. I am an American poet known for my expansive collection "Leaves of Grass," which celebrated democracy, nature, and the human spirit. My free verse broke new ground in poetry.

Who am I?

20. I am an American novelist known for my epic sea adventure "Moby-Dick." My deep and philosophical narrative explores man's struggle against nature.

Who am I?

Round 5: Master

21. I am a French writer best known for my sweeping historical novels "Les Misérables" and "The Hunchback of Notre-Dame." My works often champion the downtrodden.

Who am I?

22. I am an Italian poet known for "The Divine Comedy," an epic journey through Hell, Purgatory, and Heaven. My guide through Hell is the Roman poet Virgil.

Who am I?

23. I am an English poet best known for my epic poem "Paradise Lost," which tells the story of mankind's fall from grace and Satan's rebellion against God.

Who am I?

24. I am an American poet known for my realistic depictions of rural life and my command of American colloquial speech. My famous poem begins, "Two roads diverged in a yellow wood."

Who am I?

26. I am an English Romantic poet known for my works "Ozymandias" and "Prometheus Unbound." My passionate and revolutionary spirit was cut short when I drowned at 29.

Who am I?

Answers: Who Am I? - Famous Authors

1. William Shakespeare

Did you know? William Shakespeare known for writing 37 plays and 154 sonnets, Shakespeare's works are among the most performed in the world.

2. Homer

Did you know? Despite debates about his existence, Homer's epics remain central to Western literature.

3. Leo Tolstoy

Did you know? Tolstoy's later life was marked by his spiritual crisis and pursuit of Christian anarchism.

4. Jane Austen

Did you know? Austen's keen observations of social class and romance have made her novels timeless classics.

5. Charles Dickens

Did you know? Dickens' own experiences with poverty shaped his vivid depictions of Victorian England's social injustices.

6. Mark Twain

Did you know? Twain's sharp wit and satire made him a beloved American literary figure, and his work is still widely read today.

7. James Joyce

Did you know? Joyce's complex narrative techniques and rich use of language have made "Ulysses" one of the most challenging and rewarding reads.

8. Fyodor Dostoevsky

Did you know? Dostoevsky's exploration of the human psyche has had a profound influence on literature and psychology.

9. Gabriel García Márquez

Did you know? Márquez's masterful blending of reality and fantasy earned him the Nobel Prize in Literature.

10. Emily Dickinson

Did you know? Dickinson's innovative use of form and syntax has secured her a place as one of America's greatest poets.

11. William Faulkner

Did you know? Faulkner's intricate storytelling and exploration of Southern identity have made his works enduringly relevant.

12. Virginia Woolf

Did you know? Woolf's novels and essays have left a lasting impact on both literature and feminist thought.

13. Jorge Luis Borges

Did you know? Borges' inventive and philosophical stories continue to captivate readers and scholars alike.

14. Ernest Hemingway

Did you know? Hemingway's terse style and adventurous life have made him an iconic figure in American literature.

15. T.S. Eliot

Did you know? Eliot's deep allusions and fragmented structure in "The Waste Land" reshaped modern poetry.

16. George Orwell

Did you know? Orwell's keen political insights and powerful prose continue to resonate in discussions of freedom and oppression.

17. Franz Kafka

Did you know? Kafka's portrayal of the absurdities of modern life and bureaucracy has coined the term "Kafkaesque."

18. Edgar Allan Poe

Did you know? Poe's dark imagination and pioneering of the detective fiction genre have left an indelible mark on literature.

19. Walt Whitman

Did you know? Whitman's celebration of the individual and the collective in "Leaves of Grass" revolutionized American poetry.

20. Herman Melville

Did you know? Melville's "Moby-Dick" is a profound exploration of humanity's existential struggles.

21. Victor Hugo

Did you know? Hugo's vivid characters and social criticism in "Les Misérables" have made it a staple of world literature.

22. Dante Alighieri

Did you know? Dante's "Divine Comedy" not only tells a compelling story but also serves as a profound philosophical and theological work.

23. John Milton

Did you know? Milton's epic vision in "Paradise Lost" grapples with themes of free will, temptation, and redemption.

24. Robert Frost

Did you know? Frost's accessible yet profound poetry captures the complexities of rural New England life.

25. Percy Bysshe Shelley

Did you know? Shelley's lyrical and political intensity in his poetry continues to inspire readers and writers.

Bonus Section

Word Associations

"Words are, of course, the most powerful drug used by mankind." – Rudyard Kipling

"Words are pale shadows of forgotten names. As names have power, words have power. Words can light fires in the minds of men. Words can wring tears from the hardest hearts." – Patrick Rothfuss

"Language is the source of misunderstandings." – Antoine de Saint-Exupéry

Find the common link between - Round 1-3

Round 1: Synonym Matches

1. Cajole, Coax, Wheedle
2. Gregarious, Sociable, Outgoing
3. Laconic, Concise, Terse
4. Ponderous, Lumbering, Cumbersome
5. Melancholy, Morose, Sullen

Round 2: Category Links

1. Mercury, Venus, Mars
2. Bach, Mozart, Beethoven
3. Surrealism, Cubism, Impressionism
4. Calcium, Potassium, Sodium
5. Everest, K2, Kangchenjunga

Round 3: Word Pairs

1. Proton, Neutron
2. Keystone, Cornerstone
3. Algorithm, Heuristic
4. Synapse, Neuron
5. Keynesian, Monetarist

Answers Rounds 1-3

Round 1: Synonym Matches

1. Persuade
2. Friendly
3. Brief
4. Heavy/Slow-moving
5. Sad

Round 2: Category Links

1. Planets (inner planets)
2. Classical composers
3. Art movements
4. Elements (alkali metals)
5. Highest mountains

Round 3: Word Pairs

1. Subatomic particles
2. Important stones in architecture
3. Problem-solving methods
4. Components of the nervous system
5. Economic theories

Find the common link between - Round 4-7

Round 4: Related Terms

1. Arthropod, Mollusk, Annelid

2. Oxidation, Reduction, Combustion
3. Keynes, Friedman, Hayek
4. Sonnet, Haiku, Limerick
5. Renaissance, Baroque, Romantic

Round 5: Synonyms for Emotions

1. Apprehension, Trepidation, Foreboding
2. Vindictive, Spiteful, Malevolent
3. Enamored, Besotted, Infatuated
4. Flabbergasted, Astounded, Dumbfounded
5. Nauseated, Queasy, Bilious

Round 6: Everyday Items

1. Oscilloscope, Voltmeter, Ammeter
2. Fender, Hood, Chassis
3. Sconce, Chandelier, Pendant
4. Mortise, Tenon, Dovetail
5. Spindle, Loom, Shuttle

Round 7: Extremely Difficult Word Associations

1. Senescence, Dotage, Decrepitude
2. Anathema, Abomination, Pariah
3. Inchoate, Nascent, Rudimentary
4. Cacophony, Din, Racket
5. Encomium, Panegyric, Eulogy
6. Pellucid, Limpid, Lucid
7. Procrustean, Draconian, Exacting
8. Equanimity, Aplomb, Composure
9. Opprobrium, Ignominy, Disrepute
10. Obfuscate, Confound, Bewilder

Answers Rounds 4-6

Round 4: Related Terms

1. Invertebrates
2. Chemical reactions
3. Economists
4. Poetic forms
5. Artistic periods

Round 5: Synonyms for Emotions

1. Fear
2. Revengeful
3. Love
4. Surprised
5. Sick

Round 6: Everyday Items

1. Electrical measuring instruments
2. Car parts
3. Types of lighting fixtures
4. Woodworking joints
5. Weaving tools

Answers for Round 7: Extremely Difficult Word Associations

1. Old age/Decline
2. Something hated or despised
3. Beginning stages/Not fully formed
4. Loud, discordant noise
5. High praise
6. Clear/Transparent
7. Severely strict or harsh

8. Calmness under pressure
9. Public disgrace or shame
10. To confuse or make unclear

Bonus Section

Quotable Quest

Your task is to match the quote with the correct person. Test your knowledge and see how many you can get right!

Round 1: Quotes

1. "The only thing we have to fear is fear itself." ......
2. "I think, therefore I am." ......
3. "Injustice anywhere is a threat to justice everywhere." ......
4. "To be, or not to be, that is the question." ......
5. "The unexamined life is not worth living." ......

Match the Quote to the Person

a) William Shakespeare
b) Franklin D. Roosevelt
c) Martin Luther King Jr.
d) René Descartes
e) Socrates

Round 2: Quotes

1. "That's one small step for man, one giant leap for mankind." ......
2. "I have a dream." ......
3. "The only way to do great work is to love what you do." ......
4. "Give me liberty, or give me death!" ......
5. "I am the way, the truth, and the life." ......

Match the Quote to the Person

a) Patrick Henry
b) Martin Luther King Jr.
c) Neil Armstrong
d) Jesus Christ
e) Steve Jobs

Round 3: Quotes

1. "Float like a butterfly, sting like a bee." ......
2. "To infinity and beyond!" ......
3. "The only limit to our realization of tomorrow is our doubts of today." ......
4. "I came, I saw, I conquered." ......
5. "Elementary, my dear Watson." ......

Match the Quote to the Person

a) Muhammad Ali
b) Julius Caesar
c) Sherlock Holmes
d) Franklin D. Roosevelt
e) Buzz Lightyear

Answers - Round 1

1. b) Franklin D. Roosevelt

2. d) René Descartes
3. c) Martin Luther King Jr.
4. e) William Shakespeare
5. e) Socrates

Answers - Round 2

1. c) Neil Armstrong
2. b) Martin Luther King Jr.
3. e) Steve Jobs
4. a) Patrick Henry
5. d) Jesus Christ

Answers - Round 3

1. a) Muhammad Ali
1. e) Buzz Lightyear
2. d) Franklin D. Roosevelt
3. a) Julius Caesar
4. b) Sherlock Holmes

Round 4: Quotes

1. "An eye for an eye only ends up making the whole world blind." ......
2. "The only thing necessary for the triumph of evil is for good men to do nothing." ......
3. "Speak softly and carry a big stick; you will go far." ......
4. "Knowledge is power." ......
5. "The journey of a thousand miles begins with one step." ......

Match the Quote to the Person

a) Theodore Roosevelt
b) Lao Tzu
c) Mahatma Gandhi

d) Francis Bacon
   e) Edmund Burke

Round 5: Quotes

1. "Imagination is more important than knowledge." ......
2. "The best way to predict the future is to invent it." ......
3. "All men are created equal." ......
4. "Success is not final, failure is not fatal: It is the courage to continue that counts." ......
5. "That's one small step for man, one giant leap for mankind." ......

Match the Quote to the Person

   a) Winston Churchill
   b) Abraham Lincoln
   c) Neil Armstrong
   d) Albert Einstein
   e) Alan Kay

Round 6: Quotes

1. "You must be the change you wish to see in the world." ......
2. "The pen is mightier than the sword." ......
3. "Time is money." ......
4. "I think, therefore I am." ......
5. "The greatest glory in living lies not in never falling, but in rising every time we fall." ......

Match the Quote to the Person

   a) Nelson Mandela
   b) Mahatma Gandhi
   c) René Descartes
   d) Benjamin Franklin
   e) Edward Bulwer-Lytton

Round 7: Quotes

1. "It does not do to dwell on dreams and forget to live." ......
2. "In three words I can sum up everything I've learned about life: it goes on." ......
3. "The only thing we have to fear is fear itself." ......
4. "To be yourself in a world that is constantly trying to make you something else is the greatest accomplishment." ......
5. "Love all, trust a few, do wrong to none." ......

Match the Quote to the Person

a) Franklin D. Roosevelt
b) William Shakespeare
c) J.K. Rowling
d) Robert Frost
e) Ralph Waldo Emerson

Answers - Round 4

1. c) Mahatma Gandhi
2. e) Edmund Burke
3. a) Theodore Roosevelt
4. d) Francis Bacon
5. a) Lao Tzu

Answers - Round 5

1. d) Albert Einstein
2. e) Alan Kay
3. b) Abraham Lincoln
4. a) Winston Churchill
5. c) Neil Armstrong

Answers - Round 6

1. b) Mahatma Gandhi

2. e) Edward Bulwer-Lytton
3. d) Benjamin Franklin
4. c) René Descartes
5. a) Nelson Mandela

Answers - Round 7

1. c) J.K. Rowling
2. d) Robert Frost
3. a) Franklin D. Roosevelt
4. e) Ralph Waldo Emerson
5. b) William Shakespeare

Round 8: Quotes

1. "The future belongs to those who believe in the beauty of their dreams." ......
2. "I have not failed. I've just found 10,000 ways that won't work." ......
3. "It is never too late to be what you might have been." ......
4. "Life is what happens when you're busy making other plans." ......
5. "You miss 100% of the shots you don't take." ......

Match the Quote to the Person

a) Eleanor Roosevelt
b) Thomas Edison
c) John Lennon
d) Wayne Gretzky
e) George Eliot

Round 9: Quotes

1. "Do not go where the path may lead, go instead where there is no path and leave a trail." ......

2. "In the end, we will remember not the words of our enemies, but the silence of our friends." ......
3. "The only limit to our realization of tomorrow is our doubts of today." ......
4. "The purpose of our lives is to be happy." ......
5. "Good artists copy, great artists steal." ......

Match the Quote to the Person

   a) Pablo Picasso
   b) Martin Luther King Jr.
   c) Ralph Waldo Emerson
   d) Dalai Lama
   e) Franklin D. Roosevelt

Round 10: Quotes

1. "Happiness is not something ready-made. It comes from your own actions." ......
2. "To live is the rarest thing in the world. Most people exist, that is all." ......
3. "The only true wisdom is in knowing you know nothing." ......
4. "If you tell the truth, you don't have to remember anything." ......
5. "In the middle of difficulty lies opportunity." ......

Match the Quote to the Person

   a) Albert Einstein
   b) Mark Twain
   c) Dalai Lama
   d) Oscar Wilde
   e) Socrates

Answers - Round 8

1. a) Eleanor Roosevelt
2. b) Thomas Edison
3. e) George Eliot
4. c) John Lennon
5. d) Wayne Gretzky

Answers - Round 9

1. c) Dalai Lama
2. d) Oscar Wilde
3. e) Socrates
4. b) Mark Twain
5. a) Albert Einstein

Answers - Round 10

1. c) Ralph Waldo Emerson
2. b) Martin Luther King Jr.
3. e) Franklin D. Roosevelt
4. d) Dalai Lama
5. a) Pablo Picasso

Bonus Section

Lateral Thinking Puzzles

Try to solve each puzzle and see if you can find the surprising solutions!

Round 1: Lateral Thinking Puzzles

1. **Puzzle:** A man walks into a bar and asks the bartender for a glass of water. The bartender pulls out a gun and points it at the man. The man says "thank you" and walks out. Why? ......
2. **Puzzle:** A woman had two sons who were born on the same hour of the same day of the same year, but they were not twins. How could this be possible? ......
3. **Puzzle:** A man is found hanging in a room with no furniture and only a puddle of water below him. How did he manage to hang himself? ......
4. **Puzzle:** A man is lying dead in a field. Next to him, there is an unopened package. There are no other animals or people in the field. How did he die? ......
5. **Puzzle:** A man is driving his car, he turns on the radio, and then he dies. Why? ......

Round 2: Lateral Thinking Puzzles

1. **Puzzle:** A man was found dead in a locked room with a puddle of water around him. The windows were closed, and there was no way anyone could have entered the room. How did he die? ......

2. **Puzzle:** A woman buys a parrot. It does not speak and seems ill. When she returns it, the shopkeeper instantly knows what is wrong. How? ......
3. **Puzzle:** A man is found dead with a single hole in his shirt. There are no other injuries on his body. How did he die? ......
4. **Puzzle:** A man leaves home, makes three left turns, and returns home to find two masked men. Who are the masked men? ......
5. **Puzzle:** A man is found dead in a cabin on a mountain. How did he die? ......

Round 3: Lateral Thinking Puzzles

1. **Puzzle:** A man pushed his car. He stopped when he reached a hotel at which point he knew he was bankrupt. Why? ......
2. **Puzzle:** A man rode into town on Friday. He stayed for three nights and then left on Friday. How is this possible? ......
3. **Puzzle:** A woman shoots her husband, then holds him underwater for five minutes. Later, they both go out and enjoy a wonderful dinner together. How can this be? ......
4. **Puzzle:** A man is found dead in a telephone booth. He is soaked to the bone, and there are pieces of glass all around him. What happened? ......
5. **Puzzle:** A man is lying on the ground, dead, with a backpack on his back. What happened? ......

Answers - Round 1-3

Round 1

1. **Answer:** The man had hiccups. The bartender scared him with the gun, curing his hiccups.
2. **Answer:** They were part of a set of triplets (or more).
3. **Answer:** He stood on a block of ice to hang himself, which later melted.

4. **Answer:** The man was a parachutist. The unopened package was his parachute that failed to open.
5. **Answer:** The man was a radio DJ. He heard a song that indicated his wife was cheating on him, causing him to have a heart attack.

Round 2

1. **Answer:** The man died by hanging himself, standing on a block of ice that eventually melted.
2. **Answer:** The parrot was deaf. The shopkeeper clapped his hands to see if the parrot would react.
3. **Answer:** The man died of a gunshot wound, and the single hole in his shirt was a bullet hole.
4. **Answer:** The man was a baseball player who ran around the bases and returned home. The masked men were the catcher and the umpire.
5. **Answer:** The man died in a plane crash, and the "cabin" referred to the airplane cabin.

Round 3

1. **Answer:** The man was playing Monopoly. When he landed on a property and couldn't pay the rent, he went bankrupt.
2. **Answer:** The man's horse was named Friday.
3. **Answer:** The woman took a photograph of her husband and then developed it in the darkroom.
4. **Answer:** The man was a diver who dived into shallow water, causing the glass on the telephone booth to break and water to pour in.
5. **Answer:** The man was a skydiver, and his parachute (the backpack) failed to open.

Round 4: Lateral Thinking Puzzles

1. **Puzzle:** A man is found dead in the desert with a straw in his hand. What happened? ......

2. **Puzzle:** A man is running home. He turns a corner and sees a masked man. He turns around and runs the other way. Why? ......
3. **Puzzle:** A man is lying dead in a room with 53 bicycles scattered around him. What happened? ......
4. **Puzzle:** A man is lying dead in a cabin in the woods. There are no signs of violence. How did he die? ......
5. **Puzzle:** A man is found dead in the Arctic with a bullet wound. There are no weapons around. How did he die? ......

Round 5: Lateral Thinking Puzzles

1. **Puzzle:** A man is found dead in a room with a noose around his neck, but there is no chair or any furniture he could have stood on. How did he hang himself? ......
2. **Puzzle:** A man is found dead in a snow-covered field. There are no footprints leading to or from the body. How did he die? ......
3. **Puzzle:** A woman calls her dog and then runs away from it as fast as she can. When she stops, the dog is right in front of her. How can this be? ......
4. **Puzzle:** A man wakes up in the middle of the night, turns off the light, and goes back to bed. In the morning, he finds out that 50 people have died. How? ......
5. **Puzzle:** A man is dead in the middle of a field. The only other thing in the field is a small unopened package. What happened? ......

Round 6: Lateral Thinking Puzzles

1. **Puzzle:** A man is found dead with a piece of string in his hand. How did he die? ......
2. **Puzzle:** A man dies in his car. There are no signs of a crash or struggle. How did he die? ......

3. **Puzzle:** A woman goes into a bathroom and shoots her reflection in the mirror. She leaves the bathroom completely unharmed. How is this possible? ......
4. **Puzzle:** A man is found dead in his office. There are no wounds on his body and no signs of a struggle. How did he die? ......
5. **Puzzle:** A man lives on the 20th floor of a building. Every day he takes the elevator to the ground floor to go to work. When he returns, he takes the elevator to the 10th floor and walks the rest of the way up. Why? ......

Answers - Round 4-6

Round 4

1. **Answer:** The man drew the short straw in a life-or-death situation. He and others were stranded without enough resources, and drawing straws determined who would be sacrificed.
2. **Answer:** The man is playing baseball. The masked man is the catcher.
3. **Answer:** The man was cheating at cards. The "bicycles" refer to a brand of playing cards. He was caught and killed for cheating.
4. **Answer:** The "cabin" was an airplane cabin, and the plane crashed.
5. **Answer:** The man was shot by someone else, possibly in a remote murder. The weapon could have been removed or buried in the snow.

Round 5

1. **Answer:** He stood on a block of ice that melted.
2. **Answer:** He was dropped from an airplane.
3. **Answer:** She called the dog to her and then ran to the front door, where the dog arrived first.

4. **Answer:** He was the lighthouse keeper and turned off the light, causing a shipwreck.
5. **Answer:** He was a skydiver, and his parachute (the small unopened package) failed to open.

Round 6

1. **Answer:** The man was a puppeteer who got tangled in his puppet strings and accidentally strangled himself.
2. **Answer:** He died from carbon monoxide poisoning.
3. **Answer:** She shot the mirror, not herself.
4. **Answer:** He had a heart attack.
5. **Answer:** He is a little person who can't reach the 20th-floor button, so he takes the elevator to the 10th floor and walks up the rest of the way.

Thank You

We hope you've enjoyed unraveling the stories behind some of the most remarkable individuals who have shaped our world. Along the way, we trust you've learned some fascinating facts and gained a deeper appreciation for these icons.

Your feedback is incredibly valuable to us. If you enjoyed this book, we would greatly appreciate it if you could leave a review on Amazon. Your insights help others discover and enjoy the challenge of "Who Am I?"

As a token of our gratitude, we've prepared some exclusive free content just for you. Simply scan the QR code to unlock more intriguing trivia and challenges.

Thank you once again for being a part of this adventure. Remember, the quest for knowledge never ends—there's always more to discover, more stories to uncover, and more connections to make.

Printed in Great Britain
by Amazon